WILD BIRDS OF KOREA

Pictures and text by **Moo-Boo Yoon**
English Language Editor **G.K. Ferrar**

KYO-HAK PUBLISHING CO.

In Search of Birds

Since olden times our country has been called *Kumsu Kang-san*, silken embroidered rivers and mountains, because of its clearly distinct four seasons with each season having its own beautiful scenery. Since Korea is connected with the vast Asian continent to the north and with its east, west, and south bordered by oceans and seas, it provides good breeding areas for many migrant and resident birds.

The birds can fly freely over frontiers so their living areas are vast. Wherever we go in this country, there are birds with their buoyant bodies, their elegant plumage, and their delightful small voices. Their charm is unique; their appeal something we find in no other living things. There are delightful birds everywhere in our living environment, but it is not easy to become familiar with them even for those who have a very real interest in birds, because the birds are so swift in their flight from humans.

Recently, however, as the campaign for environmental protection has grown stronger throughout the world, concern for birds and their survival has become stronger, and the number of people interested in the status of the birds and their range has increased steadily. Bird photography is increasing which in its turn stimulates the general public's interest in them.

The author has had a strong interest in bird watching since boyhood, and in adult life has studied birds intensively, and finally has made birds the object of his academic studies and his teaching. He has taken more than 2,600 photos of over 222 species of birds over a period of twenty years, in the course of

walking around Korea from its southern tip, Mara Island, to the demilitarized zone in the north, Ch'ŏrwon, and from lonely Tok Island in the East Sea and the Kyŏknyŏlbi Archipelago, Sohŭksan Island, Kukhŭl Island and Ch'ilbal Island in the West Sea, with his research notebook.

In 1885 when ornithologist C.H.B. Tristram's thesis on Korean birds was written, there were 396 species in Korea, but he might search through a whole year throughout the country, and probably find no more than 200 species today, because some have become extinct and others no longer visit Korea. It is possible to classify Korea's original 396 species of birds as follows: 58 species of residents throughout the year, 117 species of winter visitors, 64 species of summer visitors, 103 species of transients, and 53 species of incidentals and strays. There are also some occasionals like the Crested-shelduck, family Anatidae, which was last seen in about 1940.

There are over 700 color photos of 222 species of Korean birds taken by the author included in this field guide along with information on their status, habitat, diet, range, and breeding habits.

I would like to express my appreciation to Mr. Collin Poole of BBC and Mr. Mark Eldridge, ornithologist, for their help with this English language version of *WILD BIRDS OF KOREA*

1995. 3. 14.   Moo-boo Yoon

INTRODUCTION

1. There are pictures and descriptions of 222 species of birds found in Korea in this book. They include year round residents, summer and winter residents, migratory birds, transients, and strays.
2. The names given correspond to those assigned in *Korean Birds* by the Korean Journal of Zoology, and also correspond to standard international usage.
3. The descriptions in this book include identifying features, habitat, diet, range, and breeding areas.
4. The picture captions include such relevant information as sex, season, place, and date on which the picture was taken.
5. There are a list of 396 Korean birds species and a list of those birds which have been designated natural treasures in the appendix. In the case of some of this latter group, it was impossible to get pictures, i.e. the Japanese Crested Ibis, and the turkey. Those birds, which are not preceded by a color code indicator, are year round residents.
6. For easy reference a color code is provided to indicate.
    - ● : summer resident, migratory birds
    - ● : winter resident, migratory birds
    - ● : transients
    - ○ : accidentals and strays
    - ■ : natural treasures

CONTENTS

- In Search of Birds 3
- Introduction 5

ORDER GAVIIFORMES
Family Gaviidae
  Red-throated Diver 12
  Pacific Diver 13
ORDER PODICIPEDIFORMES
Family Podicipedae
  Little Grebe 16
  Eared Grebe 18
  Great Crested Grebe 20
  Red-necked Grebe 22
ORDER PROCELLARIIFORMES
Family Procellariidae
  Streaked Shearwater 23
Family Hydrobatidae
  Swinhoe's Storm Petrel 26
ORDER PELECANIFORMES
Family Phalacrocoracidae
  Temminck's Cormorant 28
  Pelagic Cormorant 30
ORDER CICONIIFORMES
Family Ardeidae
  Bittern 31
  Chinese Little Bittern 33
  Black-crowned Night Heron 35

  Green-backed Heron 38
  Cattle Egret 40
  Chinese Egret 42
  Little Egret 45
  Intermediate Egret 48
  Great Egret 52
  Eastern Reef Heron 56
  Gray Heron 59
Family Ciconiidae
  White Stork 64
Family Threskiornithidae
  Spoonbill 68
  Black-faced Spoonbill 70
ORDER ANSERIFORMES
Family Anatidae
  Brant 71
  White-fronted Goose 74
  Swan Goose 76
  Bean Goose 77
  Mute Swan 79
  Whooper Swan 82
  Whistling Swan 87
  Ruddy Shelduck 88
  Common Shelduck 89

Mallard 92
Spot-billed Duck 96
Shoveller 100
Teal 102
Garganey 104
Baikal Teal 105
Mandarin Duck 108
Falcated Teal 112
Gadwall 114
Pintail 115
Wigeon 117
American Wigeon 119
Pochard 120
Tufted Duck 122
Greater Scaup 125
Black Scoter 129
White-winged Scoter 130
Harlequin Duck 132
Common Goldeneye 134
Smew 135
Red-breasted Merganser 137
Common Merganser 139
ORDER FALCONIFORMES
Family Accipitridae
Osprey 141
White-tailed Eagle 142
Steller's Sea-Eagle 143
Chinese Sparrow Hawk 145
Common Buzzard 146
Gray-faced Buzzard-Eagle 148
Imperial Eagle 149
Golden Eagle 150
Black Vulture 151
Northern Harrier 153
Pied Harrier 154
Marsh Harrier 155
Family Falconidae

Peregrine Falcon 156
Kestrel 157
ORDER GALLIFORMES
Family Tetraonidae
Hazel Grouse 158
Family Phasianidae
Ring-necked Pheasant 160
ORDER GRUIFORMES
Family Gruidae
Manchurian Crane 163
White-naped Crane 166
Hooded Crane 170
Family Rallidae
Ruddy Crake 174
White-breasted Waterhen 175
Common Gallinule 176
Watercock 179
Coot 181
ORDER CHARADRIIFORMES
Family Haematopdidae
Oystercatcher 183
Family Charadriidae
Little Ringed Plover 186
Long-billed Ringed Plover 189
Kentish Plover 190
Mongolian Plover 192
Lesser Golden Plover 194
Black-bellied Plover 195
Lapwing 196
Family Scolopacidae
Ruddy Turnstone 198
Rufous-necked Stint 200
Long-toed Stint 202
Sharp-tailed Sandpiper 203
Dunlin 204
Curlew Sandpiper 206
Great Knot 207

Sanderling 209
Broad-billed Sandpiper 212
Spotted Redshank 213
Redshank 216
Marsh Sandpiper 217
Greenshank 218
Wood Sandpiper 220
Gray-tailed Tattler 221
Common Sandpiper 223
Terek Sandpiper 225
Black-tailed Godwit 228
Bar-tailed Godwit 230
Australian Curlew 232
Whimbrel 234
Common Snipe 238
Family Recurvirostridae
Black-winged Stilt 240
Family Phalaropodidae
Northern Phalarope 242
Family Glareolidae
Indian Pratincole 243
Family Laridae
Black-headed Gull 245
Herring Gull 248
Slaty-backed Gull 250
Black-tailed Gull 252
Black-legged Kittiwake 257
Common Tern 260
Little Tern 262
Family Alcidae
Ancient Murrelet 265
ORDER COLUMBIFORMES
Family Columbidae
Rock Dove 267
Japanese Wood Pigeon 269
Rufous Turtle Dove 271
ORDER CUCULIFORMES
Family Cuculidae
Common Cuckoo 274
Little Cuckoo 276
ORDER STRIGIFORMES
Family Strigidae
Eagle Owl 278
Long-eared Owl 282
Short-eared Owl 283
Scops Owl 284
Collared Scops Owl 285
Brown Hawk Owl 286
Korean Wood Owl 287
ORDER APODIFORMES
Family Apodidae
White-rumped Swift 288
ORDER CORACIIFORMES
Family Alcedinidae
Black-capped Kingfisher 289
Ruddy Kingfisher 290
Common Kingfisher 292
Family Coraciidae
Broad-billed Roller 295
Family Upupidae
Hoopoe 297
ORDER PICIFORMES
Family Picidae
Gray-headed Woodpecker 300
Black Woodpecker 301
White-bellied Black Woodpecker 304
Great Spotted Woodpecker 307
White-backed Woodpecker 308
Dagelet White-backed Woodpecker 310
Gray-headed Pygmy Woodpecker 312
Japanese Pygmy Woodpecker 314
ORDER PASSERIFORMES
Family Pittidae
Fairy Pitta 316

Family Alaudidae
Skylark 317
Family Hirundinidae
Bank Swallow 318
House Swallow 319
Red-rumped Swallow 323
Family Motacillidae
Forest Wagtail 325
Yellow Wagtail 326
Gray Wagtail 328
White-faced Wagtail 330
White Wagtail 333
Pied Wagtail 334
Japanese Wagtail 335
Indian Tree Pipit 337
Water Pipit 338
Family Pycnonotidae
Brown-eared Bulbul 340
Family Laniidae
Thick-billed Shrike 343
Bull-headed Shrike 345
Brown Shrike 347
Northern Shrike 348
Family Bombycillidae
Bohemian Waxwing 350
Japanese Waxwing 352
Family Troglodytidae
Winter Wren 354
Family Muscicapidae
Subfamily Turdinae
Siberian Bluechat 356
Pied Wheatear 358
Daurian Redstart 359
Stonechat 362
Blue Rockthrush 364
White's Ground Thrush 365
Gray-backed Thrush 366
Pale Thrush 367
Dusky Thrush 368
Naumann's Thrush 370
Subfamily Paradoxornithnae
Vinous-throated Parrotbill 372
Subfamily Sylviinae
Bush Warbler 375
Island Grasshopper Warbler 377
Great Reed Warbler 378
Arctic Warbler 380
Pale-legged Willow Warbler 381
Subfamily Muscicapinae
Tricolor Flycatcher 382
Blue and White Flycatcher 384
Family Aegithalidae
Long-tailed Tit 385
Family Paridae
Marsh Tit 386
Coal Tit 387
Varied Tit 388
Great Tit 390
Family Sittidae
Nuthatch 392
Family Zosteropidae
Japanese White-eye 394
Family Emberizidae
Siberian Meadow Bunting 398
Japanese Reed Bunting 400
Tristram's Bunting 401
Gray-headed Bunting 403
Little Bunting 405
Rustic Bunting 406
Yellow-throated Bunting 408
Chestnut Bunting 410
Siberian Black-faced Bunting 412
Reed Bunting 413
Family Fringillidae

Brambling 414
Oriental Greenfinch 416
Siskin 419
Scarlet Finch 420
Pallas' Rosy Finch 421
Long-tailed Rose Finch 423
Bullfinch 424
Chinese Grosbeak 425
Hawfinch 428
Family Ploceidae
Russet Sparrow 429
Tree Sparrow 431
Family Sturnidae
Daurian Myna 433
Gray Starling 435
Family Oriolidae
Black-naped Oriole 438

Family Corvidae
Jay 441
Azure-winged Magpie 443
Black-billed Magpie 445
Rook 450
Carrion Crow 451

■ APPENDIX
Korean Birds Designated Natural Treasures, Their Breeding Areas, Habitats 457
Korean Birds 396 Species 499
Scientific Names 539
English Names 543
References 547

Wild Birds of Korea

Prof. Moo-boo Yoon

Red-throated Diver. Kyŏngp'o Lake, Kangwon Province. 1992. 1. 26.

Red-throated Diver at rest. 1992. 1. 26.

Order Gaviiformes/Family Gaviidae

Red-throated Diver •

Gavia stellata
Korean · Abi   63cm

Sexes similar. Winter: white face, chin, neck, breast; white speckles on gray-brown back and nape. Summer: red throat patch; gray cheeks, gray neck.
STATUS: Relatively rare winter visitor.
HABITAT: Harbors, along coast, inland on fresh water reservoirs, lakes, alone or with Pacific Loon.
DIET: Fish, shellfish.
RANGE: Arctic, Alaska, Aleutian Islands, northern England.

Pacific Diver in search of a school of anchovies. Kŏje Island. 1992. 2. 1.

Order Gaviiformes/Family Gaviidae

Pacific Diver ●

Gavia Pacifica
Korean · Hoisaekmŏriabi   65cm

Good swimmer and diver. Sexes similar. Winter : gray-brown head and back ; white throat and breast. Summer : white head; gray-brown back speckled white with white stripes; throat blue.
STATUS : Common winter visitor.
HABITAT : Along coasts often mixing with Arctic Loons in groups of 2 or 3 to thousands of birds.
DIET : Fish, shellfish, molluscs, echinoderms.
RANGE : Breed from northern Siberia to Alaska, Canadian Arctic and Pacific coast.

Pacific Divers in winter. Kŏje Island. 1992. 2. 1.

Pacific Divers in search of anchovies. Kŏje Island. 1992. 2. 1.

Little Grebe in summer. Asan Lake. 1990. 6. 21.

Order Podicipediformes/Family Podicipedae

Little Grebe •

Podiceps ruficollis
Korean · Nonbyŏngari　　　　26cm

Little Grebe eggs in nest. 1990. 6. 21.

Good diver. Sexes similar. Summer: black head and back; dark brown breast and belly; rufous cheeks. Winter: dark brown head and back; the rest pale brown.
STATUS : Common winter visitor.
HABITAT : Rivers, reservoirs, along coast; some groups build nests floating on water in reeds and brush on inland rivers, lakes and ponds.
DIET : Fish, shellfish, insects, seeds.
RANGE : Northeast China, Japan, and Kuril Archipelago; winters from Korea to the Ryukyus.

Little Grebe in search of fish. Asan Lake. 1990. 6. 21.

Eared Grebe in winter plumage. Kangwon Province. 1983. 1. 16.

Order Podicipediformes/Family Podicipedae

Eared Grebe •

Podiceps nigricollis
Korean · Kŏmŭnmoknonbyŏng-ari   33cm

Good swimmer and diver. Sexes similar. Winter : black-brown head, neck and back ; lower cheeks and belly white. Summer : black head, neck, back, rufous abdomen, yellowish ear feathers.
STATUS : Common winter visitor.
HABITAT : Southern sea coast ; large flock on Kŏje Island coast.
DIET : Fish, shellfish, molluscs, insects.
RANGE : Warm regions of Eurasia from Ussuri to Manchuria in Asia ; winters in China, Korea, and Japan.

Eared Grebes in winter. Ŭlsuk Island, Naktong River. 1989. 1. 2.

Summer. Kyŏngp'o Lake. 1990. 4. 28.   Winter. Kyŏngp'o Lake. 1990. 1. 10.

Order Podicipediformes / Family Podicipedae

Great Crested Grebe ●

Podiceps cristatus
Korean • Pulnonbyŏngari   56cm

Sexes similar. Winter: black crest; dark brown neck and back; white throat and belly. Summer: crest and sides of neck black; white cheeks, neck and belly; dark brown back; red at base of crest.
STATUS : Winter visitor.
HABITAT : Along coast, lakes, rivers. Often swims with back under water and neck held low; neck held straight when in danger.
DIET : Fish, amphibians, molluscs, water insects, reed buds.
RANGE : Warm regions of Asia, all Europe, northern latitudes of Siberia; winters in Korea, South China, Japan.

Male and female courting. Kyŏngp'o Lake, Kangwon Province. 1984. 1. 11.

Great Crested Grebes. Kyŏngp'o Lake, Kangwon Province. 1990. 2. 3.

Red-necked Grebe in winter. Kŏje Island. 1991. 2. 20.

Order Podicipediformes/Family Podicipedae

Red-necked Grebe •

Podiceps grisegena
Korean • Kŭnnonbyŏngari   47cm

Sexes similar. Good swimmer and diver. Winter: top of head, neck, back, wings black-brown; cheeks, breast, belly white. Summer: rufous neck; light gray cheeks.
STATUS : Rare winter visitor.
HABITAT : Winters alone or male and female together among Pacific or Arctic Loons in harbors on sea in winter, not inland.
DIET : Fish, frogs, shellfish, water insects.
RANGE : Kamchatka Peninsula, eastern Siberia, Manchuria, Sakhalin, Hokkaido, North America; winters in Korea and in temperate zone.

Streaked Shearwater on eggs. Sasu Island, Wando-gun, Chŏllanam Province. 1983. 8. 6.

Order Procellariiformes/Family Procellariidae

Streaked Shearwater •

Calonectris leucomelas
Korean • Sŭmsae   48cm

Swims in groups, gathers in large numbers after sunset in breeding area. Sexes similar. Black-gray head and back; white face, neck, belly; many white spots on face and head; whitish gray bill.
STATUS : Summer visitor.
HABITAT : Breeds on Ullŭng Island, Ch'ilbal Island, Kukhŭl Island.
DIET : Fish, molluscs, seaweed mainly.
RANGE : From northern islands of Hokkaido to coast of southern Ryukyus, coast of China; winters in the Philippines or further south.

Streaked Shearwater on nest. 1991. 8. 13.

Streaked Shearwater egg in nest. 1991. 8. 13.

Flock of Streaked Shearwaters searching for food. Chŏllanam Province. 1991. 8. 14.

Swinhoe's Storm Petrel on nest. Kukhŭl Island, Shinan-gun, Chŏllanam Province. 1991. 8. 13.

Order Procellariiformes/Family Hydrobatidae

Swinhoe's Storm Petrel ●

Oceanodroma monorhis
Korean • Patajebi   19cm

Sexes similar. Dark brown body; light brown on wing coverts; bill and legs black.
STATUS : Summer visitor.
HABITAT : Uninhabited islands, such as Tok Island in East Sea and Ch'ilbal and Kukhŭl Islands in Yellow Sea.
DIET : Fish, shellfish, molluscs, plankton.
RANGE : China, Taiwan; winters in Singapore, Sumatra, Java and south to Indian coast.

Baby bird. Ch'ilbal Island. 1990. 8. 3.

Ch'ilbal Island. Shinan-gun, Chŏllanam Province.
Female on nest. Ch'ilbal Island. 1990. 8. 3. ▶

Temminck's Cormorants at rest. Kŏje Island. 1990. 2. 24.

Temminck's Cormorants on rocks.

Order Pelecaniformes/Family Phalacrocoracidae

Temminck's Cormorant •

Phalacrocorax filamentosus
Korean • Kamauji   84cm

Sexes similar. Winter : whole body glossy blue-black; yellow face. Summer : white head and legs.
STATUS : Winter visitor.
HABITAT : Alone or in groups on coasts and rivers; searches for prey by diving or by swimming with neck above water and body and tail under water. Common on Naktong River estuary, Sŏngsanp'o on Cheju Island and on uninhabited islands off southeast coast.
DIET : Fish.
RANGE : Ussuri, northern coast of China, Japan, Taiwan.

Temminck's Cormorants drying feathers after diving. Sŏngsanp'o, Cheju Island. 1989. 1. 2.

Temminck's Cormorants on coast. Sŏngsanp'o, Cheju Island. 1987. 2. 3.

Pelagic Cormorants in winter. Kŏje Island. 1992. 2. 26.

Order Pelecaniformes/Family Phalacrocoracidae

Pelagic Cormorant ●

Phalacrocorax pelagicus
Korean · Soegamauji   73cm

Sexes similar. Good swimmer and diver. Whole body black with glossy green ; green eyes with exposed skin around eyes red in summer, brown in winter.
STATUS : Winter visitor.
HABITAT : Found in groups of 2 or 3 to 20 or 30 ; mixes with fresh water Temminck's Cormorant ; on lakes, rivers, estuaries, harbors, reefs along coast or seaside.
DIET : Fish, shellfish.
RANGE : Chukot Peninsula, Kamchatka Peninsula, Komandor Island, Sakhalin, Kuril Archipelago, northern Japan, Alaska ; winters in Korea, Japan, Taiwan.

Order Ciconiiformes/Family Ardeidae

Bittern •

Botaurus stellaris
Korean • Allakhaeoragi   70cm

Sexes similar. Whole body yellowish brown; vertical dark brown stripes on belly, neck, and breast; black crown; note peculiar pattern on back.

STATUS: Very rare summer visitor.
HABITAT: Found in tall grass and in lakes, marshes in southern Kyŏnggi Province, reeds on Kyŏngp'o Lake in Kangwon Province and marshes in Sinhori, Naktong River estuary in winter. When enemy appears, it holds bill straight up to look like a reed.
DIET: Fish, rats, frogs, shrimp.
RANGE: Europe, China, Siberia, northern Japan.

Bittern disguising itself as reed. Kyŏngp'o Lake, Kangwon Province. 1990. 3. 30.

Chinese Little Bittern searching for food in rice field. Kyŏnggi Province. 1990. 9. 2.

Order Ciconiiformes / Family Ardeidae

Chinese Little Bittern ●

Ixobrychus sinensis
Korean・Tŏmbulhaeoragi　　36cm

Sexes similar. Dark brown head, wings, and tail; yellowish brown on wing coverts, neck and belly; cheeks and sides of neck red. Female : vertical rufous stripes on neck and belly.
STATUS : Rare summer visitor.
HABITAT : Breeds only in isolated marshes; seen in pairs or solitary in marshes or rice fields; seeks food at dusk.
DIET : Fish, frogs, shellfish.
RANGE : Northeastern Manchuria, Japan, Sakhalin, Taiwan; winters in India, Sri Lanka, Malaysia, Philippines.

◄ Bittern in reeds. Kyŏngp'o Lake, Kangwon Province. 1992. 3. 6.

Chinese Little Bittern searching for food in reeds. Anyang, Kyŏnggi Province. 1990. 6. 20.

◄ Chinese Little Bittern eggs in nest.

Female Black-crowned Night Heron. P'yŏngtaek, Kyŏnggi Province. 1991. 6. 20.

Order Ciconiiformes/Family Ardeidae

Black-crowned Night Heron •

Nycticorax nycticorax
Korean · Haeoragi 57cm

Sexes similar. Glossy black with blue-green head and back; white cheeks, neck, breast, belly and two plumes on head; black bill; dark yellow legs.
STATUS : Summer visitor.
HABITAT : A few in central Korea; spends daytime in rice fields, lakes, marshes, reeds; searches for food mainly at night.
DIET : Fish, shrimp, frogs, snakes, rodents, insects.
RANGE : Japan, Sakhalin, Eurasia, Africa; winters in Taiwan, Philippines, Malaya Peninsula, Indo-China.

Female Black-crowned Night Heron on eggs.

Black-crowned Night Heron eggs in nest.

Black-crowned Night Heron in flight. Kimp'o. 1992. 6. 28.

Young Black-crowned Night Heron. 1992. 6. 28.   Male Black-crowned Night Heron. 1991. 6. 20.
◄ Male Black-crowned Night Heron. Kimp'o, Kyŏnggi Province. 1992. 6. 28.

Male Green-backed Heron searching for food in rice fields. Kyŏnggi Province. 1986. 5. 29.

Baby Green-backed Heron. 1987. 8. 20.

Order Ciconiiformes/Family Ardeidae

Green-backed Heron •

Butorides striatus
Korean · Kŏmŭndaenggihaeoragi
52cm

Sexes similar. Gray with black head; light gray body; white vertical stripe on neck; black plume.
STATUS: Summer visitor.
HABITAT: All over Korea near villages, lakes, reservoirs, streams, rivers, valleys; alone and in pairs.
DIET: Small fish, frogs, shellfish, water insects.
RANGE: Lower Amur River, Ussuri, eastern Manchuria, Japan; winters in Philippines, Borneo.

Male Green-backed Heron feeding in rice field. Kŏje Island. 1988. 6. 5.

Cattle Egrets in flight. Kŏje Island. 1990. 6. 6.

Cattle Egret on eggs. 1990. 7. 5.

Baby Cattle Egrets and eggs. 1992. 6. 6.

Order Ciconiiformes/Family Ardeidae

Cattle Egret •

Bubulcus ibis
Korean • Hwangno   50.5cm

Sexes similar. Body white; rufous head, breast, and belly; yellow bill; dark brown legs.
STATUS : Summer visitor.
HABITAT : 50 pairs a year breed in Ch'ungch'ŏngnam Province, Kangwon Province, Kyŏnggi Province; appears around May on central area riversides, reservoirs, downstream of rivers and marshes near rice fields.
DIET : Insects, frogs, fish.
RANGE : India, Myanmar, Japan, Philippines; winters in Ryukyus, Philippines.

Cattle Egrets on guard near nest. Kimp'o, Kyŏnggi Province. 1992. 6. 28. ▶

Female and male Chinese Egrets at rest. Shin Island, Kyŏnggi Province. 1991. 6. 20.

Order Ciconiiformes/Family Ardeidae

Chinese Egret ●

Egretta eulophotes
Korean · Norangburibaekno 65cm

Sexes similar. Whole body white; green between eye and bill; more than twenty 8cm plumes; yellow bill and feet.
STATUS : Summer visitor, endangered species.
HABITAT : Nesting area Shin Island, Ongjin-gun, Kyŏnggi Province; rare on Kanghwa Island in Kyŏnggi Province and on western coastal islands. Internationaly protected bird.
DIET : Fish, shellfish.
RANGE : Warm regions of eastern Asia, Ussuri, Manchuria, eastern China, reported nesting in Japan and Taiwan.
■ Natural Treasure No. 361.

Chinese Egret at rest. Shin Island, Ongjin-gun, Kyŏnggi Province. 1991. 6. 20.

Shin Island, Ongjin-gun, nesting area for Chinese Egrets. 1991. 6. 20.

Chinese Egrets, seacoast. Miruji, Kanghwa-gun, Kyŏnggi Province. 1988. 6. 2.

Baby Chinese Egret and egg. Shin Island, Ongjin-gun, Kyŏnggi Province. 1991. 6. 20.

Little Egret stalking prey, seacoast. Miruji, Kanghwa-gun, Kyŏnggi Province. 1988. 6. 2.

Order Ciconiiformes/Family Ardeidae

Little Egret ●

Egretta garzetta
Korean · Soebaekno　　　　61cm

Sexes similar. Black bill and legs; yellow feet; all white body; two plumes on back of head.
STATUS : Summer visitor from middle of April
HABITAT : Nests in Kamsŏngni, Yŏngi-gun, Ch'ungch'ŏng-nam Province, Ap'kokni, Hoengsŏng-gun, Kangwon Province; found along riversides, reservoirs, and shallow shore areas.
DIET : Fish, frogs, snakes, shellfish, water insects.
RANGE : China, Japan, Taiwan, Hainan Island, Indo-China, Myanmar, India, southern Europe, Africa, Madagaskar.

Twelve day old Little Egrets. 1992. 6. 28.

Male Little Egret preening. Kimp'o. 1992. 6. 28.

Little Egret guarding nest. Kimp'o, Kyŏnggi Province. 1992. 6. 28.

Little Egrets in search of food. Ŭlsuk Island in Naktong River. 1986. 9. 10.

Mother feeding her nestlings. Kamsŏngni, Yŏngi-gun, Ch'ungch'ŏngnam Province. 1989. 6. 5.

Order Ciconiiformes/Family Ardeidae

Intermediate Egret •

Egretta intermedia
Korean • Chungbaekno   68.5cm

Sexes similar. Whole body white; bill black from center to tip; bill base yellow; black legs.
STATUS : Summer visitor.

HABITAT : Nests in central Korea in small concentrated groups; feeds in rice fields, on riversides, in marshes, nests thicker than Great Egrets; lives on ground except during mating and nesting periods.
DIET : Fish.
RANGE : From tropics to temperate zone of Asia, India, Japan, Philippines; winters in Taiwan and Philippines.

Intermediate Egret in forest. Kimp'o, Kyŏnggi Province. 1992. 6. 28. ▶

Mother Intermediate Egret shading nestlings. Yŏju, Kyŏnggi Province. 1989. 6. 6.

Intermediate Egrets. 1989. 6. 6.

Young Intermediate Egrets. 1989. 6. 6.

Intermediate Egrets nesting. Kamsŏngni, Yŏngi-gun, Ch'ungch'ŏngnam Province. 1989. 6. 6.

Young Great Egrets. Mogokni, Hongch'ŏn-gun, Kangwon Province. 1990. 7. 5.

Great Egret by nest. 1992. 7. 30.

Order Ciconiiformes/Family Ardeidae

Great Egret ●

Egretta alba
Korean・Chungdaebaekno   90cm

Sexes similar. Whole body white; black bill and legs; vivid green skin just below eyes.
STATUS : Common summer visitor.
HABITAT : Breeds countrywide; lives on ground except during mating and nesting periods; searches in rice fields, streams and marshes for food; breeds in groups with Gray Herons and Little Egrets in forests of pine, ginkgo, and bamboo.
DIET : Fish, frogs, tadpoles, rats.
RANGE : Manchuria, China.

Great Egrets after mating. Yŏju, Kyŏnggi Province. 1991. 6. 21.

Young Great Egret. Mogokni, Hongch'ŏn-gun, Kangwon Province. 1991. 7. 21.

Eastern Reef Heron on the wing. Sŏgwip'o, Cheju Island. 1992. 6. 6.

Eastern Reef Heron. 1992. 6. 6.

Order Ciconiiformes/Family Ardeidae

Eastern Reef Heron

Egretta sacra
Korean • Hŭkno   62cm

Sexes similar. Black bill; yellow legs; whole body gray-black with some dark brown.
STATUS : Resident.
HABITAT : Uninhabited islands on hidden rocks; builds plate shaped nest on reefs on uninhabited islands or in trees or on cliffs of such islands.
DIET : Fish, crabs, shellfish.
RANGE : From eastern tropics of Asian coast to Australian Pacific coast and islands, Myanmar, Malay coast, southern Japan, northern Australia, New Zealand, Taiwan.

Eastern Reef Heron on coast. Cheju Island. 1990. 1. 10.

Gray Heron carrying nest building materials. Ch'unch'ŏn, Kangwon Province. 1990. 4. 5.

Order Ciconiiformes/Family Ardeidae

Gray Heron •

Ardea cinerea
Korean · Oegari 90cm

Sexes similar. Whole body light to dark gray; two long black plumes; vertical spotted pattern on throat; black shoulders; reddish yellow bill.
STATUS : Common summer visitor.
HABITAT : Breeds in all areas of Korea; some groups winter over in central and southern areas, seem to have become resident birds; nest in big trees and build nests in higher places than Egrets which breed at same time.
DIET : Fish, frogs, snakes, rats, shrimp, insects, crawfish, small birds.
RANGE : Japan, eastern China, Mongolia, Indo-China, Myanmar.

◄ Gray Heron breeding area. Mogokni, Hongch'ŏn-gun, Kangwon Province. 1991. 3. 16.

Brooding female Gray Heron. Mogokni, Hongch'ŏn-gun, Kangwon Province. 1991. 3. 16.

Gray Herons in nesting area. Ch'unch'ŏn, Kangwon Province. 1990. 4. 5.

Mating Pair of Gray Herons. Ap'kokni, Hoengsŏng-gun, Kangwon Province. 1990. 3. 1.

Twenty day old Gray Herons. Yŏngi-gun, Ch'ungch'ŏngnam Province. 1989. 6. 6.

Gray Heron pair at sunset. Kamsŏngni, Yŏngi-gun, Ch'ungch'ongnam Province. 1989. 6. 6.

Female White Stork. Ŭmsŏng-gun, Ch'ungch'ŏngbuk Province. 1974. 5. 30.

Order Ciconiiformes/Family Ciconiidae

White Stork •

Ciconia ciconia
Korean • Hwangsae   112cm

Sexes similar. Whole body white; bill and back of wings brilliant black; red legs and around eyes.
STATUS : Rare winter visitor.
HABITAT : Rivers, lakes and marshes in central and southern areas; live beside lakes on estuaries, marshes, rice fields, alone or in small groups.
DIET : Freshwater plants, fish, frogs, shrews, spiders, insects, rice plant roots.
RANGE : Siberia, southern Yŏnhaeju, southern China.
■ Natural Treasure No. 199.

Flying White Stork. Cheju Island 1988. 1. 7.

Widow White Stork's egg. 1974. 5. 30.

Widow White Stork. Ŭmsŏng-gun, Ch'ungch'ŏngbuk Province. 1974. 5. 30. ▶

Flock of White Storks in flight from North Korea: largest number at that time. Kapch'ŏn,

vicinity of Taejŏn, Ch'ungch'ŏngnam Province. 1976. 10. 20.

Spoonbills on the wing among flock of geese. Chunam Reservoir, Ch'angwon. 1992. 1. 18.

Order Ciconiiformes/Family Threskiornithidae

Spoonbill •

Platalea leucorodia
Korean • Norangburijōsae   86cm

Sexes similar. Summer : tip of bill and upper breast yellow ; bill and legs black ; rest of plumage white. In winter breast white ; yellow becomes less on bill tip.
STATUS : Very rare winter visitor.
HABITAT : Marshes, shallow lakes, rivers, seaside, island reefs and sand ; searches for food by moving bill from side to side in shallow water.
DIET : Small fish, frogs, tadpoles, shellfish, insects, freshwater plants.
RANGE : Southern Europe, Mediterranean Sea environs, India, Sri Lanka, Mongolia, Manchuria, Ussuri.
■ Natural Treasure No. 205.

Spoonbills in search of food. Chunam Reservoir, Ch'angwon. 1994. 1. 5.

Black-faced Spoonbills on coast. Sŏngsanp'o, Cheju Island. 1986. 1. 20.

Order Ciconiiformes/Family Threskiornithidae

Black-faced Spoonbill ●

Platalea minor
Korean・Chŏŏsae   73.5cm

Sexes similar. Whole body white; black bill and legs. Winter: back of head and neck yellow.
STATUS : Rare winter visitor and passage migrant.

HABITAT : Coast of Kanghwa Island, Naktong River estuary, Cheju Island; recently confirmed to breed on uninhabited islands in Yellow Sea; lives in shallow coastal waters, tideland swamps, marshes, reed fields.
DIET : Small freshwater fish, frogs, tadpoles, shellfish, insects and freshwater plants.
RANGE : Central Manchuria, eastern China, Japan, Taiwan, Indo-China; winters in Korea.
■ Natural Treasure No. 205.

Group of Brants at rest downstream. Ŭlsuk Island, Naktong River. 1987. 12. 30.

Order Anseriformes/Family Anatidae

Brant •

Branta bernicla
Korean · Hŭkkirŏgi   61cm

Sexes similar. Black breast, head, back; belly white with lateral black stripes; white patch with black lateral stripes on neck; black legs and feet.
STATUS : Rare winter visitor.
HABITAT : South seacoast islands regularly; solitary or in small groups; rests at high tide and at night on surface of sea; searches for food at low tide line and in shallow coastal water.
DIET : Seaweed, shellfish.
RANGE : From Arctic region of eastern Siberia to western tundra of Canada; winters in Korea, Japan, China, west coast of North America.

Brant in search of food. 1987. 12. 30.

■ Natural Treasure No. 325.

Brants on the wing downstream. Ŭlsuk Island, Naktong River. 1987. 12. 30.

Order Anseriformes/Family Anatidae

White-fronted Goose •

Anser albifrons
Korean • Soegirŏgi   72cm

Sexes similar. Dark brown head; grayish brown neck and back; breast and belly gray with black pattern; white forehead; bill pink and legs yellow.
STATUS : Winter visitor.
HABITAT : Throughout Korea except east coast and mountains; found in rice and dry fields, marshes, reclaimed land, estuaries, broad open regions; spends daytime in harbors, on lakes and ponds, in reclaimed areas in groups; searches for food in fields in morning and evening.
DIET : Grass, leaves, stalks, roots, green leaves of wheat or barley, grass in marshes and along coasts.
RANGE : Alaska, eastern Siberian tundra, western America, Japan.

White-fronted Geese on the wing. Chunam

White-fronted Geese at rest on reservoir. Kyŏngsangnam Province. 1986. 1. 4.

Reservoir, Kyŏngsangnam Province. 1992. 1. 18.

White-fronted Geese searching for food in rice field. Kyŏngsangnam Province. 1992. 1. 18.

Swan Geese searching for food. Chunam Reservoir, Kyŏngsangnam Province. 1992. 1. 18.

Order Anseriformes/Family Anatidae

Swan Goose ●

Anser cygnoides
Korean · Kaeri　　　　　　　87cm

Sexes similar. Dark brown from front of eyes upper head and along back of neck; dark brown back and wings, gray brown and blackish stripes; front of neck belly pale buffish brown; white to yellowish cheeks; gray-brown breast.
STATUS: Relatively rare winter visitor.
HABITAT: In small groups on lakes and ponds, in rice fields, marshes, on grassy land, along coasts, on reclaimed land.
DIET: Water plants, rice and barley plants, wheat, shellfish.
RANGE: Downstream of Amur River, Kamchatka Peninsula; winters in Korea.
■ Natural Treasure No. 325.

Bean Geese. Chunam Reservoir, Ch'angwon, Kyŏngsangnam Province. 1992. 1. 18.

Order Anseriformes/Family Anatidae

Bean Goose •

Anser fabalis
Korean • Kŭngirŏgi   85cm

Sexes similar. Dark brown head and back; brown belly; orange legs and feet; black bill with vivid yellow band around center.
STATUS : Next most common winter visitor after White-fronted Goose.

HABITAT : Spends winters everywhere except mountainous regions ; searches for food along coast in reclaimed areas, rice fields and dry fields, marshes, lakes and ponds ; in groups on rivers and streams in broad open areas.
DIET : Green leaves of wheat and barley, other cereals ; corn, wheat, barley, potatoes, sweet-potatoes.
RANGE : Siberian tundra, Arctic, northern Mongolia, temperate zone.

Bean Geese on the wing. Chunam Reservoir, Kyŏngsangnam Province. 1990. 12. 26.

Bean Geese. Ŭlsuk Island, Naktong River. 1983. 1. 21.

Mute Swans. Chumunjin Lake, Kangwon Province. 1981. 1. 12.

Order Anseriformes/Family Anatidae

Mute Swan •

Cygnus olor
Korean • Hokkoni   152cm

Sexes similar. Almost whole body white; orange bill; black bump in front of eyes; black legs. Young gray-brown over whole body.
STATUS : Very rare winter visitor.
HABITAT : Kyŏngp'o Lake, on marshes, lakes and ponds.
DIET : Water plants, small animals.

Mute Swan. Ch'ŏngch'o Lake. 1987. 1. 3.

RANGE : Northern Europe, eastern Siberia, Ussuri basin; winters in northern Africa, southwestern Asia, northwestern India, Japan.

Female Mute Swans (white) and young Mute Swans (dark) in winter. Sokch'o. 1987. 1. 3.

Whooper Swans on Chumunjin Lake, Kangwon Province. 1987. 1. 3.

Order Anseriformes/Family Anatidae

Whooper Swan •

Cygnus cygnus
Korean • Kŭngoni   140cm

Whooper Swans feeding. 1988. 12. 11.

Sexes similar. Whole body white; black bill and legs; yellow between bill and eyes; young gray to shades of black.
STATUS: Winter visitor.
HABITAT: Along coast toward south in reservoirs, water-filled rice fields, lakes and ponds, marshes, estuaries; lives on surface of shallow water in family groups male, female, and young.
DIET: Stalks and roots of water plants, grass seeds, marine insects.
RANGE: Northern Europe, Siberia, northwestern Manchuria, valley of Amur, northern Ussuri, Sakhalin; winters in Mediterranean and Black Sea areas, Japan.
■ Natural Treasure No. 201.

Whooper Swans rising to fly. Changnim, Naktong River. 1992. 12. 12.

Whooper Swans rising to fly. Kyŏngp'o Lake, Kangwon Province. 1992. 1. 22.

Whooper Swans feeding on grass and roots. Kangnŭng, Kangwon Province. 1992. 1. 22.

Whistling Swan in winter on Ch'ŏngch'o Lake, Sokch'o, Kangwon Province. 1982. 1. 30.

Order Anseriformes/Family Anatidae

Whistling Swan •

Cygnus columbianus
Korean • Koni   120cm

Sexes similar. White body, black bill and legs; base of bill yellow; smaller than Whooper Swan.
STATUS: Rare winter visitor.

HABITAT: Mixed in very small numbers with Whooper Swans; lives mainly on lakes, ponds, marshes, rivers, and streams, coastal areas.
DIET: Similar to Whooper Swan.
RANGE: Siberian tundra, at edges of pine forests; winters in northern Europe, coast of China, Japan.
■ Natural Treasure No. 201.

◄ Whooper Swans in search of food at dawn. Kyŏngsangbuk Province. 1987. 12. 24.

Ruddy Shelducks on frozen Han River. 1972. 1. 5.

Order Anseriformes/Family Anatidae

Ruddy Shelduck •

Tadorna ferruginea
Korean · Hwangori   63.5cm

Ruddy Shelduck. 1972. 1. 5.

Sexes similar. Whole body orange ; front of wings white ; black on wings ; tail and legs black ; black band on male's neck ; female's face white.
STATUS : Common winter visitor along coast in small and large flocks, but recently decreasing in number.
HABITAT : Marshes, lakes, and ponds, grassy fields, rivers and streams, tidelands, rice fields and dry fields.
DIET : Cereals, barley, wheat and millet, rotten fish.
RANGE : Temperate zone of Eurasia, northern Africa, Mongolia, northern India, southern China, Japan.

Common Shelducks on the wing downstream on Naktong River. 1985. 1. 16.

Order Anseriformes/Family Anatidae

Common Shelduck •

Tadorna tadorna
Korean · Hokpuriori   62.5cm

Sexes similar. Head and back of wings black with glossy green; wide light brown band on breast; red bill, legs, and feet; rest white.
STATUS : Winter visitor.
HABITAT : Ŭlsuk Island in Naktong River estuary, Asan Bay region; in groups of 10 to 700 together mainly on reclaimed land along coast.
DIET : Small fish, water insects, seaweed, snails.
RANGE : Siberian tundra, Europe, northern Baikal Lake region; winters in Korea, Japan, southern China, northern Africa.

Group of Common Shelducks in search of food.

Common Shelducks in search of food. Ülsuk Island, Naktong River. 1989. 1. 28.

Male and female Mallard in search of food. Kangwon Province. 1987. 2. 1.

Order Anseriformes/Family Anatidae

Mallard ●

Anas platyrhynchos
Korean · Ch'ŏngdungori   64cm

Male : iridescent green head ; narrow white ring on neck ; chestnut brown breast ; rest light gray.
Female : brown-black head ; body dark brown mixed with black.
STATUS : Common winter visitor.
HABITAT : Coast, fields, marshes, ponds, rivers, and streams in flocks in winter but scatters for mating in spring.
DIET : Grass seeds, fruits, insects, invertebrates.
RANGE : Arctic and temperate zones ; winters in temperate and subtropical zones.

Mallard pair on Ch'ŏngch'o Lake.

Male and female Mallards. Hwajinp'o, Kosŏng-gun, Kangwon Province. 1992. 2. 26.

Mallards feeding on water plants. Hwajinp'o, Kosŏng-gun, Kangwon Province. 1992. 2. 26.

Mallards in search of rice in snow covered field. Ch'orwon, Kangwon Province. 1992. 2. 3.

Spot-billed Duck on Han River. 1980. 1. 13.

Order Anseriformes/Family Anatidae

Spot-billed Duck

Anas poecilorhyncha
Korean · Hinpyamgŏmdungori
60.5cm

Sexes similar. Black with rufous body; black striped cheeks; white eye stripe; black bill with yellow tip; speculum blue.
STATUS : Resident; breeds on Bam Island, Han River, Seoul.
HABITAT : Rivers and streams, marshes, ponds, uninhabited islands.
DIET : Grass seeds, fruits, insects, invertebrates.

Spot-billed Duck eggs. 1980. 6. 4.

RANGE : Amur River, southern Sakhalin, Japan, China, southern Asia.

Spot-billed Ducks on Bam Island. Han River, Seoul. 1983. 1. 18.

Male and female Spot-billed Duck in rice field. Kyŏnggi Province. 1983. 4. 10.

Spot-billed Ducks. Ülsuk Island, Naktong River. 1987. 2. 18.

Shovellers in winter on Chunam Reservoir. Kyŏngsangnam Province. 1992. 2. 20.

Order Anseriformes/Family Anatidae

Shoveller •

Anas clypeata
Korean · Nŏpchŏkpuri   50cm

Male : head glossy green ; white breast ; orange legs and feet ; chestnut belly ; black back and bill. Female : whole body yellowish brown mixed with red-brown ; orange legs.

STATUS : Common winter visitor.
HABITAT : Central and southern areas ; small flocks on ground or beside water in marshes ; large flocks on sea ; rests in daytime on quiet seas or on lakes and ponds, estuaries, and marshes ; active at night in search of food.
DIET : Reeds, invertebrates.
RANGE : From Arctic to temperate zone, northern Europe, Siberia ; winters in Korea, Japan, Taiwan.

Shovellers resting. Chunam Reservoir, Changwon, Kyŏngsangnam Province. 1992. 2. 20. ▶

Male Teal. Ch'ŏngch'o Lake, Sokch'o. 1992. 1. 17.

Order Anseriformes/Family Anatidae

Teal •

Anas crecca
Korean • Soeori　　　　　　37.5cm

Male : chestnut head with broad blue-green patch from eyes to base of neck ; light black-brown body with white stripe on side. Female : whole body yellowish brown.
STATUS : Common winter visitor.
HABITAT : Lakes, ponds, reservoirs, rivers, estuaries throughout Korea ; in flocks separate from other ducks ; daytime in flocks in large numbers resting on lakes, surface of sea, tilled areas, any safe place at night ; look for food in rice fields, dry fields, marshes, reed beds, stream sides.
DIET : Seeds, reeds, beetles, invertebrates.
RANGE : Europe, Siberia to northern Manchuria, Japan ; winters in Korea, Philippines.

Male and female Teal in search of food. Ch'ŏngch'o Lake, Sokch'o. 1992. 1. 7.

Teals at rest. Ch'ŏngch'o Lake, Sokch'o. 1992. 1. 7.

Male Garganeys wintering on reservoir. Sŏngsanp'o, Cheju Island. 1985. 12. 31.

Order Anseriformes/Family Anatidae

Garganey •

Anas querquedula
Korean · Palguji   38cm

Male : red-brown head, small spotted pattern on neck and cheeks ; white line curves over eyes to nape ; yellowish brown scale pattern on breast ; white, brown, black stripes on back. Female : yellowish brown ; dark brown pattern over whole body.

STATUS : Rare winter visitor and passage migrant.

HABITAT : Lakes, marshes, rivers and streams, bays, rice fields ; sometimes mountainous regions to 800m in Kimhae in Kyŏngsangnam Province or Chinjŏp-myŏn, Namyangju-gun, Kyŏnggi Province, Hadori on Cheju Island.

DIET : Rice, grass seeds, water insects.

RANGE : Subarctic and temperate zone.

Order Anseriformes/Family Anatidae

Baikal Teal •

Anas formosa
Korean · Kach'angori 40cm

Male : top of head black ; pinkish gray breast ; belly gray with black stripes ; unusual green, yellow, black facial pattern. Female : black and reddish brown body.
STATUS : Winter visitor.
HABITAT : In large flocks of tens of thousands of birds ; lakes, marshes, rice fields.
DIET : Grass seeds, cereals, rice.
RANGE : Eastern Siberia, Amur River, northern Sakhalin ; winters in Korea, Japan, China.

Baikal Teal in search of food. Chunam Reservoir, Kyŏngsangnam Province. 1987. 2. 3.

Flock of Baikal Teals on the wing at twilight. Kyŏngsangnam Province. 1988. 2. 13.

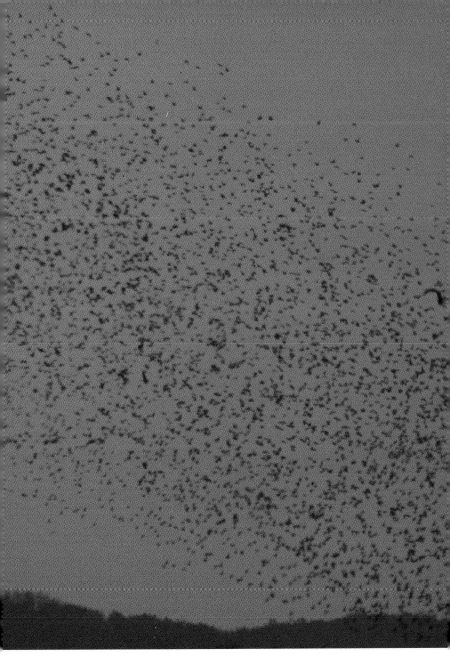

Male Mandarin Duck. Kwangnŭng, Kyŏnggi Province. 1991. 12. 21.

Order Anseriformes/Family Anatidae

Mandarin Duck

Aix galericulata
Korean · Wonangi   45cm

Male : chestnut head ; two vertical stripes on breast sides ; olive-brown back ; face and plume orange-rufous. Female : dark gray with pattern of white spots on whole body.
STATUS : Rare resident.
HABITAT : Breeds in crevices in walls and in holes in forest trees ; lives in large or small flocks in marshes, lakes, ponds.
DIET : Grass seeds, fruit, snails, small freshwater fish.
RANGE : Siberia, eastern temperate zone, Ussuri, China, Japan.
■ Natural Treasure No. 327.

Male and two females on tree branch. Kwangnŭng, Kyonggi Province. 1988. 2. 26. ▶

Flock of Mandarin Ducks in winter in forest. Kwangnŭng Kyŏnggi Province. 1991. 12. 21.

Male Falcated Teal. Nanjido, Han River, Seoul. 1972. 2. 25.

Order Anseriformes/Family Anatidae

Falcated Teal •

Anas falcata
Korean • Chŏngmŏriori   48cm

Male : iridescent brown head; blue-green from eyes to nape; body light gray speckled with black; clear black band on neck.
Female : dark brown speckled with yellow-brown.
STATUS : Rare winter visitor.
HABITAT : Downstream on Naktong River, Chunam Reservoir, coastal areas, lakes and ponds, marshes, grassland, rice fields, rivers, and streams.
DIET : Cereals, grass seeds, leaves and roots, water insects, and small invertebrates.
RANGE : Eastern Siberia, Amur River, Ussuri, Mongolia, Sakhalin, Hokkaido; winters in Korea, Japan, North America.

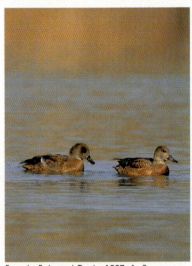
Female Falcated Teals. 1987. 1. 3.

Male and female Falcated Teal. Kyŏngsangnam Province. 1988. 1. 16.

Male and female Gadwall. Tanch'ŏn, Han River, Seoul. 1978. 1. 23.

Order Anseriformes/Family Anatidae

Gadwall •

Anas strepera
Korean • Allakori　　　　　50cm

Male and female Gadwall. 1988. 2. 1.

Male : brown head ; end of tail black ; mottled light gray and black over whole body ; black bill. Female : whole body yellowish brown and mottled brown ; orange bill.
STATUS : Winter visitor in small groups.
HABITAT : Lakes and ponds, swamps, marshes, grassland near ponds ; in flocks separate from other duck species ; seen with Coots on P'aldang Lake.
DIET : Reeds, water insects.
RANGE : All northern Europe, south temperate zone and Arctic ; winters in North America, Korea, India.

Pintail in winter on reservoir near sea. Sŏngsanp'o, Cheju Island. 1990. 2. 9.

Order Anseriformes/Family Anatidae

Pintail ●

Anas acuta
Korean · Kobangori
75cm (male)   53cm (female)

Male : chocolate-brown head and back of neck; long pointed black tail feathers; light gray and black body; white throat with white extending up side of neck; black under tail coverts with cream colored band at sides of ventral area. Female : whole body yellowish brown.
STATUS : Common winter visitor.
HABITAT : Winters mixed with Mallards and other species in bays, lakes, streams, marshes, swamps, rice fields; large flocks rest on surface of sea during day, and search for food in rice fields and marshes until dawn.
DIET : Small grain cereals, roots of reeds, vegetables, invertebrates.
RANGE : From temperate zone to subarctic, Europe, Siberia; winters in India, Korea, Japan.

Pintails on Bam Island on Han River. 1972. 1. 20.

Group of Pintails with other ducks. Ŭlsuk Island, Naktong River. 1985. 12. 25.

Male and female on lake in winter. Sŏngsanp'o, Cheju Island. 1990. 2. 9.

Order Anseriformes/Family Anatidae

Wigeon •

Anas penelope
Korean · Hongmŏriori   48cm

Wigeon droppings. 1990. 2. 9.

Male : brown head, cream color at top ; gray-black line down back ; rufous breast ; white belly.
Female : light brown.
STATUS : Common winter visitor.
HABITAT : Winters in bays, on reclaimed land, in estuaries, on lakes and ponds, rice fields, grasslands.
DIET : Aquatic plants, reeds, invertebrates.
RANGE : Northern Europe, Siberia, Kamchatka ; winters in India, Korea, Sakhalin.

Male Wigeons on the wing. Sŏngsanp'o, Cheju Island. 1990. 2. 9.

Wigeons at rest. Sŏngsanp'o, Cheju Island. 1990. 2. 9.

American Wigeon in winter. Sŏngsanp'o, Cheju Island. 1982. 1. 23.

Order Anseriformes/Family Anatidae

American Wigeon ○

Anas americana
Korean · Amerikahongmŏriori
48cm

Male : cream colored head with many black spots ; blue-green band from eyes to back of neck ; white crown ; brown breast and flanks, white belly. Female : yellow-brown head, dark brown back.
STATUS : Very rare winter visitor ; stray bird.
HABITAT : Rests in marshes and in grass and bushes from sunset to dawn ; seeks food in rice fields in daytime ; on lakes and marshes, sometimes mixes with Wigeons.
DIET : Reeds, seeds, water insects, shellfish.
RANGE : Subarctic, North America ; winters in California.

Pochard in winter. Bam Island, Han River, Seoul. 1984. 1. 13.

Order Anseriformes/Family Anatidae

Pochard •

Aythya ferina
Korean • Hinjukchi   45cm

Male : brownish red head ; black breast and tail ; gray-white with small pattern on body. Female : light chestnut head and breast ; light brown hook shaped patterns back of eyes ; gray bill.
STATUS : Common winter visitor.

HABITAT : Winters in large flocks mixed with Tufted Ducks in marshes, ponds, rivers and streams, estuaries ; numbers have increased in Han River since reclamation work.
DIET : Leaves and stalks of reeds, fruits, marine invertebrates.
RANGE : Siberia from subarctic to the temperate zone, northern Europe, Black Sea, Baikal Lake, Sakhalin ; winters in Europe, India, Korea, Japan.

Flock of Pochards on lake. Hwajinp'o, Kosŏng-gun, Kangwon Province. 1992. 2. 21.

Male and female Tufted Duck in winter. Kangwon Province. 1978. 1. 22.

Order Anseriformes/Family Anatidae

Tufted Duck ●

Aythya fuligula
Korean · Taenggihinjukchi 40cm

Male : glossy black except white belly, black drooping crest from back of head. Female : whole body dark brown with light brown stripes ; bill gray-blue.
STATUS : Common winter visitor ; lives in groups of 3 to 5 birds, or flocks of 400 to 500 birds.
HABITAT : Lakes, ponds, surface of sea, swamps, estuaries, on inland waters ; leaps in an arc before diving.
DIET : Larva of aquatic insects, molluscs, shellfish, grass seeds.
RANGE : From subarctic to the temperate zone, Siberia ; winters in Korea, India, China.

Female Tufted Ducks on river. Myŏngji, Naktong River. 1986. 1. 26.

Tufted Ducks on the wing. Myŏngji, Naktong River. 1988. 2. 13.

Tufted Ducks in winter. Myŏngji, Naktong River. 1988. 2. 12.

Male Greater Scaup in winter. Myŏngji. Naktong River, 1988. 2. 12.

Order Anseriformes/Family Anatidae

Greater Scaup •

Aythya marila
Korean · Kŏmŭnmŏrihinjukchi
45cm

Greater Scaup in flight. 1988. 2. 12.

Male : glossy dark blue-green head, breast, tail ; gray back with light patterns ; white belly. Female : dark brown head, breast, back ; white belly and white between eyes and bill.
STATUS : Winter visitor.
HABITAT : South especially on Naktong River and along south coast, in freshwater lakes, estuaries, bays and along coast in flocks of 100 to ten thousand birds.
DIET : Molluscs, shellfish, small fish, marine insects.
RANGE : Eurasia, Arctic on North American continent ; winters in eastern Siberia, Kamchatka Peninsula, Kuril Archipelago, Korea, Japan, China.

Flock of Greater Scaups in winter. Ülsuk Island, Naktong River. 1988. 2. 12.

Black Scoters on the wing. Ŭlsuk Island, Naktong River. 1988. 2. 13.

Order Anseriformes/Family Anatidae

Black Scoter •

Melanitta nigra
Korean • Kŏmdungori   48cm

Male : whole body glossy black ; bill yellowish orange at base.
Female : whole body dark brown ; dark cream cheeks and under chin ; dark gray bill.
STATUS : Common winter visitor.
HABITAT : South and east coasts on sea or in estuaries ; in pairs or in groups of 10.
DIET : Shellfish, molluscs, invertebrates.
RANGE : Eastern Siberia, west coast of Alaska, Aluetian Archipelago, California ; winters in Korea, Japan, China.

◄ Black Scoters on the coast. Bongp'o, Kosŏng-gun, Kangwon Province. 1988. 2. 13.

White-winged Scoters. Ülsuk Island, Naktong River. 1989. 1. 13.

Order Anseriformes/Family Anatidae

White-winged Scoter •

Melanitta fusca
Korean · Kŏmdungorisach'on 55cm

Male: glossy black; white crescent under eyes and white secondaries; orange bill. Female: dark brown; pale patches on face.
STATUS: Common winter visitor.
HABITAT: Winters in southern sea and East Sea, estuaries, big rivers and streams, along coasts, in reservoirs; a diver; increasing in Naktong River estuary since construction of dam on estuary.
DIET: Shellfish, molluscs.
RANGE: Eastern Siberia, Altai, Minsk; winters in Kamchatka, northern Kuril Archipelago, Korea, Japan, China.

Flock of White-winged Scoters. Ülsuk Island,

Male White-winged Scoter. Ůlsuk Islands, Naktong River. 1989. 1. 13.

Naktong River. 1989. 1. 13.

Female Harlequin Ducks. Ayajin, Kosŏng-gun, Kangwon Province. 1987. 12. 6.

Order Anseriformes/Family Anatidae

Harlequin Duck ●

Histrionicus histrionicus
Korean • Hinjulbagiori 43cm

Male : dark blue head, back, breast ; white pattern on sides of head, neck, and breast ; reddish brown belly. Female : whole body dark brown ; about 3 white spots on head ; gray bill.
STATUS : Winter visitor.
HABITAT : South and east coasts on reefs and rocks.
DIET : Small fish, molluscs, shellfish, crabs.
RANGE : Arctic, eastern Siberia, Baikal Lake, Sakhalin, Kuril Archipelago ; winters in northeastern America, Korea.

Male Harlequin Ducks on east coast. Kosŏng-gun, Kangwon Province. 1987. 12. 6.

Male Common Goldeneye. Kohyŏn, Kŏje Island. 1976. 1. 8.

Order Anseriformes/Family Anatidae

Common Goldeneye •

Bucephala clangula
Korean • Hinpyamori   45cm

Male: glossy blue-green head; middle of back black; white sides, belly, neck; white patch under eye. Female: chestnut head; dark brown back, brown breast and belly; bill tip orange.
STATUS : Winter visitor.
HABITAT : East and south coasts, rivers and ponds, lakes; lives mainly on sea in groups of 3~5 up to 100 birds; good swimmer and diver.
DIET : Insects, shellfish.

Common Goldeneye on the wing.

RANGE : Winters in Europe on coasts and northern India, Korea, southern China, Taiwan.

Male Smew. Bam Island, Han River, Seoul. 1976. 1. 8.

Order Anseriformes/Family Anatidae

Smew •

Mergus albellus
Korean • Hinbiori   42cm

Male: white with black on face and down center of back, shoulders, tail and sides. Female: cheeks, chin white; chestnut head; dark brown back; gray breast and belly with brown stripes.

STATUS: Rare winter visitor.
HABITAT: Prefers big rivers and streams, forests along rivers, reservoirs; alone or two together; good diver; in winter lives in rivers and streams, along coast, estuaries, reservoirs, lakes and ponds.
DIET: Fish, molluscs, shellfish.
RANGE: Northern Scandinavia, northern Siberia, eastern Siberia; winters in Europe, Caspian Sea, Korea, Japan.

Pochard at rest with Smew. Bam Island, Han River. 1990. 1. 8.

A group of female smews at rest on lake. Kangwon Province. 1985. 2. 1.

Male Red-breasted Merganser on the wing. Kangwon Province. 1985. 1. 9.

Order Anseriformes/Family Anatidae
Red-breasted Merganser •

Mergus serrator
Korean • Padabiori   55cm

Male Red-breasted Merganser. 1989. 2. 18.

Male: glossy greenish brown head; crest, shoulders and back black; white collar; brown band on breast. Female: whole body dark gray; rufous head.
STATUS: Common winter visitor.
HABITAT: Winters along south coast; lives around reefs in groups of 5~12 birds; dives in calm areas for food.
DIET: Fish, shrimp, crabs.
RANGE: Arctic to subarctic; winters in Kamchatka, Korea, China, Japan, California, Europe.

Group of Red-breasted Mergansers on south coast. Kŏje Island. 1989. 2. 18.

Red-breasted Mergansers. Sokch'o, Kangwon Province. 1983. 1. 3.

Male and female Common Merganser in search of food. Seoul. 1990. 12. 29.

Order Anseriformes/Family Anatidae

Common Merganser •

Mergus merganser
Korean · Piori   65cm

Male: glossy blue-green head; black down center of back; cream colored breast. Female: rufous head; white under chin and neck; gray with dark brown belly and back.
STATUS : Common winter visitor.
HABITAT : Reservoirs, lakes, rivers and streams, ponds; dives for fish in shallow water; lives in flocks.
DIET : Fish, marine insects.
RANGE : Northern Europe, Siberia, Kamchatka Peninsula, central Europe, central Russia; winters in Mediterranean, Black Sea, Caspian Sea areas, northern India, Korea, Japan.

Female Common Merganser.

Male Common Merganser.

Common Mergansers resting on Bam Island. Han River, Seoul. 1990. 12. 29.

Osprey on the wing. Miruji, Kanghwa-gun, Kyŏnggi Province. 1989. 10. 15.

Order Falconiformes/Family Accipitridae

Osprey •

Pandion haliaetus
Korean • Mulsuri
54cm (male) 64cm (female)

Osprey. Ch'ŏngch'o Lake. 1985. 10. 1.

Sexes similar. Top of head, neck, belly white; black-brown eye stripe and back of head; dark brown breast; tail lighter on underside.
STATUS : Winter visitor.
HABITAT : South and Cheju Island; during migratory season lives along coasts, on estuaries, big reservoirs; eats and rests in trees by water.
DIET : Fresh and salt water fish.
RANGE : Eurasia, northern Africa, Siberia; winters in India, Africa, southeastern Asia, Philippines.

White-tailed Eagle on the wing. Songji Lake, Kosŏng-gun, Kangwon Province. 1987. 12. 6.

Order Falconiformes/Family Accipitridae

White-tailed Eagle •

Haliaeetus albicilla
Korean • Hinkorisuri
80cm (male)　95cm (female)

Sexes similar. Yellowish brown head, shoulders; brown breast, belly, back; dark brown wings; white tail; yellow bill and feet.
STATUS : Rare winter visitor.
HABITAT : Rocks along coasts; swamps, marshes, inland lakes, rivers and streams, estuaries, reclaimed land; not in mountains; lives alone.
DIET : Salmon, trout, rabbits, rats, ducks, snipe, crows, water fowl.
RANGE : Siberia, subarctic and temperate zones, northern Europe.
■ Natural Treasure No. 243.

Young bird. Han River, Seoul. 1986. 12. 5.

Order Falconiformes/Family Accipitridae

Steller's Sea-Eagle •

Haliaeetus pelagicus
Korean • Chamsuri
88cm (male)   102cm (female)

Sexes similar. Whole body dark brown; white forehead, shoulders, tail; big bill; feet yellow.
STATUS : Very rare winter visitor.
HABITAT : Along coasts, downstream on rivers and streams, mountainous areas, lakes and marshes; alone or in groups with 5 or 6 Black Vultures and White-tailed Eagles.
DIET : Salmon, trout, rabbits, seaweed, fish, rotten meat.
RANGE : Kamchatka Peninsula, Amur River, Sakhalin; winters in Ussuri, Korea, Hokkaido.
■ Natural Treasure No. 243.

Steller's Sea-Eagle on the wing. Ŭlsuk Island, Naktong River. 1989. 1. 17.

Steller's Sea-Eagle taking off. Ŭlsuk Island, Naktong River. 1989. 1. 17.

Steller's Sea-Eagle at rest. Ŭlsuk Island, Naktong River. 1989. 1. 17.

Chinese Sparrow Hawk watching for prey. Kap'yŏng-gun, Kyŏnggi Province. 1990. 6. 25.

Order Falconiformes/Family Accipitridae

Chinese Sparrow Hawk •

Accipiter soloensis
Korean · Pulgŭnbaesaemae
27cm (male) 30cm (female)

Sexes similar. Gray head, back, tail; white belly; light rufous under chin, on breast; black on underside of wing tip; yellow bill base.

STATUS : Common summer visitor.

HABITAT : All areas of central Korea; flat lands, hills, oak trees, pine trees near villages.

DIET : Frogs, small fowl.

Chinese Sparrow Hawk eggs. 1983. 7. 2.

RANGE : Eastern Asia from temperate zone to subtropics, from southern Manchuria to China.
■ Natural Treasure No. 323.

Common Buzzard. Kwangnŭng, Kyŏnggi Province. 1984. 1. 8.

Order Falconiformes/Family Accipitridae

Common Buzzard

Buteo buteo
Korean · Maltonggari   54cm

Sexes similar. Yellowish brown with dark brown on head, breast; dark brown under chin, back; white belly; yellow-brown tail, underside of wings.
STATUS : Common resident.
HABITAT : Farms, cities, hills in suburbs, rivers, coasts, mountainous areas; summer in deep forest in remote areas; alone or male and female together; eat on branch of old tree or stake.
DIET : Rodents, fowl, amphibians, reptiles, insects.
RANGE : Siberia, temperate and Arctic zones.

Common Buzzard on the wing.

Common Buzzard watching for prey. Sadong, Ullŭng Island. 1990. 8. 19. ▶

Gray-faced Buzzard-Eagle rarely seen in Yellow Sea area. Kyŏnggi Province. 1984. 3. 25.

Order Falconiformes/Family Accipitridae

Gray-faced Buzzard-Eagle ●

Butastur indicus
Korean · Wangsaemae 49cm

Sexes similar. Dark brown head, back, tail; blackish gray cheeks, chin, wing edges, tail stripe; white eyebrow; yellow feet; white with dark brown horizontal pattern on belly.
STATUS : Common transient in spring and autumn, some winter visitors, mostly summer visitor.
HABITAT : Alone or in pairs ; rest on tree branches.
DIET : Rodents, snakes, amphibians, locusts, small birds.
RANGE : Temperate zone of eastern Asia, southern Amur River, Ussuri, Japan, Manchuria, China.

Order Falconiformes/Family Accipitridae

Imperial Eagle •

Aquila heliaca
Korean • Hinjukchisuri   82cm

Sexes similar. Yellow-brown head and back of neck; rest dark brown; brown wings and tail edges; young bird's body yellow-brown; yellow-brown pattern on wings.

STATUS : Rare winter visitor.
HABITAT : Not active, rests on trees or rocks for long periods; more like Common Buzzard than Black Vulture; usually solitary but sometimes in small groups like Black Vulture.
DIET : Insects, birds, small mammals, carrion.
RANGE : Central Siberia, temperate zone; winters in Iran, northern India, China, Korea.

Imperial Eagle on bank. Ilsan, Kyŏnggi Province. 1985. 2. 22.

Golden Eagle over forest in search of food. Yanggu, Kangwon Province. 1989. 8. 23.

Order Falconiformes/Family Accipitridae

Golden Eagle

Aquila chrysaetos
Korean · Kŏmdoksuri   85cm

Sexes similar. Top of head, back of neck yellow-brown; rest dark brown; yellow-brown pattern on center of wings; underside center of wings, also tail of young birds white.
STATUS : Resident.
HABITAT : Lives inland on rock cliffs; moves down coast and rivers; estuaries near sea coast, reclaimed land.
DIET : Small mammals, medium sized birds.
RANGE : Northern temperate zone, Japan, Europe.
■ Natural Treasure No. 243.

Black Vulture wintering in estuary. Ŭlsuk Island, Naktong River. 1983. 1. 6.

Order Falconiformes/Family Accipitridae

Black Vulture •

Aegypius monachus
Korean • Toksuri   102~112cm

Sexes similar. Whole body blackish, dark brown; pale gray-brown on neck; base of bill and feet gray-green.

STATUS : Rare winter visitor.
HABITAT : Solitary or male and female or 5~6 birds together; near big rivers, lakes, swamps, marshes, estuaries.
DIET : Carrion, weak ducks, water fowl.
RANGE : Temperate zone, Mediterranean Sea, prairies, waste lands, high alpine regions.
■ Natural Treasure No. 243.

Black Vulture in winter. DMZ, Ch'ŏrwon-gun, Kangwon Province. 1994. 1. 20.

Northern Harrier in search of prey. Ŭlsuk Island, Naktong River. 1983. 2. 8.

Order Falconiformes/Family Accipitridae

Northern Harrier ●

Circus cyaneus
Korean · Chaetpitkaegurimae
  43cm (male) 53cm (female)

Male : gray head, breast, back, tail ; white belly ; black wing tips. Female : whole body brown with dark brown spots ; black wing tips ; white waist.
STATUS : Common winter visitor.
HABITAT : Alone, reclaimed land, marshes, isolated hill areas, grassland, along rivers, tilled lands.
DIET : Rodents, birds.
RANGE : Except American continent, from temperate to arctic zones ; winters in Korea, Japan, Iran, India, Myanmar, China.
■ Natural Treasure No. 323.

Pied Harrier in search of prey. in P'anmunjŏm. 1984. 8. 21.

Order Falconiformes/Family Accipitridae

Pied Harrier ●

Circus melanoleucos
Korean · Allakkaegurimae   45cm

Male : black head, back, wings ; white lesser wing coverts, belly ; rest of wings, back and tail gray.
Female : similar to female Northern Harrier ; dark gray wing edges, tail.
STATUS : Rare transient, seen in demilitarized zone.
HABITAT : Rivers, grassy places near forests.
DIET : Small fowl, frogs, fish.
RANGE : Amur River area, Manchuria, North Korea ; winters in China, Philippines, Borneo, India.

Male Pied Harrier. 1984. 8. 21.

Marsh Harrier in search of prey. Ch'ŏrwon, Kangwon Province. 1989. 10. 28.

Order Falconiformes/Family Accipitridae

Marsh Harrier •

Circus aeruginosus
Korean · Kaegurimae
48cm (male) 58cm (female)

Male : dark brown or black head ; gray or black wings, back, white breast and belly. Female : light brown almost pink-beige head, breast ; rufous back, wings, belly.

STATUS : Transient in spring and autumn.

HABITAT : Flies over fields at 1~2m in search of prey ; usually sits on ground or grass ; rests on stakes or rocks, never in tall trees ; usually alone.

DIET : Rats, fowl, amphibians, reptiles.

RANGE : Eastern Siberia, northern Mongolia, Amur River, Ussuri, Sakhalin, Hokkaido.

Peregrine Falcons with prey Teal. Sŏngsanp'o, Cheju Island. 1988. 2. 1.

Order Falconiformes/Family Falconidae

Peregrine Falcon

Falco peregrinus
Korean · Mae   51cm

Sexes similar. Dark gray head, cheeks, back; white under chin; dirty white breast, belly with black horizontal pattern; young birds have spotted pattern on breast.
STATUS : Rare resident.
HABITAT : Cliffs on coasts and islands; solitary; dives on prey very fast with wings closed and grabs it with claws.
DIET : Small birds.
RANGE : Eastern Siberia, coast of Okhotsk Sea, Kamchatka, Sakhalin, Japan, Taiwan.
■ Natural Treasure No. 323.

Kestrel in search of prey. Hongch'ŏn, Kangwon Province. 1974. 3. 20.

Order Falconiformes/Family Falconidae

Kestrel

Falco tinnunculus
Korean · Hwangjorongi
　　　30cm (male)　33cm (female)

Male: gray head, rump and tail; black vertical lines under eyes; black and white lines on tip of tail; rufous back with black spots; black edged wings; cream colored belly with black spots; black primaries. Female: rufous with black spots on head, tail, breast, and back.

Eggs. 1986. 5. 11.

STATUS: Resident throughout the country.
HABITAT: Lives in cities, villages, rural districts, on cliffs beside rivers, and between walls of buildings; alone or male and female together.
DIET: Field rats, moles, reptiles, small fowl.
RANGE: Japan, China, Myanmar.
■ Natural Treasure No. 323.

Hazel Grouse in search of food. Kwangnŭng, Kyŏnggi Province. 1992. 3. 12.

Order Galliformes/Family Tetraonidae

Hazel Grouse

Tetrastes bonasia
Korean・Tŭlkwŏng   36cm

Male : gray-brown head, back, tail with dark brown stripes ; black chin ; white breast and belly with rufous bars. Female : dark brown head, back, tail ; white chin with red-brown bars ; both male and female have red wattle above eyes.
STATUS : Resident.
HABITAT : In summer male and female remain together on ground in leaf covered areas, in trees.
DIET : Berries, leaves, flowers, seeds, insects.
RANGE : Siberia, Amur, Sakhalin, Manchuria, Japan, Hokkaido.

Hazel Grouse in shrubbery. Yŏngwol-gun, Kangwon Province. 1992. 3. 1. ▶

Male Ring-necked Pheasant in breeding season. Kyŏnggi Province. 1986. 6. 25.

Order Galliformes / Family Phasianidae

Ring-necked Pheasant

Phasianus colchicus
Korean · Kwŏng
   80cm (male)   60cm (female)

Male : brown top of head, tail ; red cheeks ; blue-green neck with white ring ; rufous breast and belly ; yellowish gray-brown back. Female : mottled brown and black.
STATUS : Common resident.
HABITAT : Breeds throughout country in park areas and cities, old palaces ; hills in rural and seaside areas ; forests except on remote islands.
DIET : Seeds of Graminaceae grasses, grain, berries, insects, spiders.
RANGE : Northern Mongolia, Ussuri, Manchuria, Japan.

Female Ring-necked Pheasant.

Ring-necked Pheasant in winter plumage. Kwangnŭng, Kyŏnggi Province. 1981. 1. 7.

Male Ring-necked Pheasant on snow. Kwangnŭng, Kyŏnggi Province. 1981. 1. 7.

Male Ring-necked Pheasant in winter plumage. Chŏngnŭng. Seoul. 1970. 2. 3.

Male Ring-necked Pheasant eating grass seeds. Kyŏngsangnam Province. 1992. 6. 24.

Manchurian Crane. Ch'ŏrwon, Kangwon Province. 1986. 1. 17.

Order Gruiformes/Family Gruidae

Manchurian Crane •

Grus japonensis
Korean · Turumi   140cm

Sexes similar. Red cap; black chin, neck, primaries; rest of body white; black legs; yellow-brown bill; young rufous.

STATUS : Rare winter visitor.

HABITAT : West central area of DMZ, Ch'ŏrwon area, Taesong-dong, P'anmunjŏm vicinity, near night soil disposal plant in northern Inch'ŏn. In family groups on fields.

DIET : Fresh water fish, locusts.

Manchurian Cranes in search of food.

RANGE : Northeastern Hokkaido, Hayrungchang Sŏng in China.
■ Natural Treasure No. 202.

Group of Manchurian Cranes, White-naped Cranes and Bean Geese in DMZ in winter.

Ch'ŏrwon, Kangwon Province 1992. 1. 5.

White-naped Cranes in search of food. Ch'ŏrwon(DMZ), Kangwon Province. 1992. 1. 5.

Order Gruiformes/Family Gruidae

White-naped Crane ●

Grus vipio
Korean · Chaedurumi　　　127cm

Sexes similar. Red around eyes with black border; white back of head, under chin, back of neck; dark gray throat, breast, back, belly; light gray front of wings; head of young birds reddish brown.
STATUS: Rare winter visitor.
HABITAT: Mud along inlet banks, estuaries, marshes, and in fields, idle land, in groups of 50 to 300 birds with male, female and 2 or 3 young in family groups during winter.
DIET: Fish, shellfish, rice plants, plant roots.
RANGE: From Khanka Lake in Siberia to Mongolia and Manchuria.
■ Natural Treasure No. 203.

White-naped Cranes on the wing. Munbalri, P'aju-gun, Kyŏnggi Province. 1987. 2. 26.

White-naped Cranes on the wing. Ch'ŏrwon, Kangwon Province. 1992. 1. 19.

White-naped Cranes feeding on inlet bank in winter. Kimp'o, Kyŏnggi Province. 1983. 1. 23.

Hooded Cranes wintering in rice field. Talsŏng-gun, Kyŏngsangbuk Province. 1992. 2. 21.

Order Gruiformes/Family Gruidae

Hooded Crane ●

Grus monacha
Korean · Hŭkturumi   96.5cm

Sexes similar. Black lower forehead, red cap; gray-black breast, belly, back; white neck, head; black legs. Young have brown heads.

STATUS : Rare winter visitor in Kyŏnggi Province, Kyŏngsangbuk Province, Kangwon Province.

HABITAT : In groups in rice fields and dry fields, shallow rivers and streams.

DIET : Fish, shellfish, insects, rice and barley plants, roots of Graminaceae grasses.

RANGE : Amur River to Manchuria in small groups.

■ Natural Treasure No. 228.

Hooded Cranes feeding on grain in rice field. Kyŏngsangbuk Province. 1992. 2. 21. ▶

Hooded Cranes on the wing. Talsŏng-gun, Kyŏngsangbuk Province. 1992. 2. 21.

Ruddy Crake walking on pond in search of food. Kwangju, Kyŏnggi Province. 1986. 7. 2.

Ruddy Crake eggs. 1987. 7. 12.

Order Gruiformes/Family Rallidae

Ruddy Crake •

Porzana fusca
Korean • Soetŭmbugisach'on
22.5cm

Sexes similar. Red-brown head, breast, upper belly; brown back; lower belly has white stripes; red legs; dark gray bill.

STATUS: Common summer visitor.

HABITAT: Found throughout country in marshes, rice fields, grass and bushes; when frightened lowers head and tail and runs into high grass; searches for food in high grass; walks on floating water plants.

DIET: Insects, frogs, blowfish seeds of Graminaceae grasses.

RANGE: Southern Manchuria, eastern China, Japan; winters in Indo-China, Myanmar, Thailand.

White-breasted Waterhen. Anyang, Kyŏnggi Province. 1987. 6. 25.

Order Gruiformes/Family Rallidae

White-breasted Waterhen ●

Amaurornis phoenicurus
Korean · Hinbaetŭmbugi   32.5cm

Sexes similar. Back of head, back dark brown; lower belly red; white cheeks, neck, breast, upper belly; yellowish brown legs; yellow bill with red at base.
STATUS : Rare transient along west coast in spring and autumn.
HABITAT : Rice fields, marshes, lakes and ponds, ditches, near areas of high grass, in reeds near waterways; runs on ground bobbing tail.

White-breasted Waterhen.

DIET : Insects, shellfish, cereals.
RANGE : From western Pakistan to northern India, Myanmar, China.

Common Gallinule in search of food in reeds. Ch'ungch'ŏngnam Province. 1988. 6. 6.

Order Gruiformes/Family Rallidae

Common Gallinule ●

Gallinula chloropus
Korean · Soemuldak   32.5cm

Sexes similar. Black with short, white lines on sides; two white spots under tail; base of bill and forehead red; tip of bill and feet yellow.

STATUS : Relatively common summer visitor.

HABITAT : Estuaries, rivers and streams, lakes and ponds, swamps, reservoirs, reeds in waterways, rice fields, especially among reeds and water plants; hides in shallow areas in reeds

DIET : All sorts of seeds, insects, berries, molluscs, shellfish, annelid.

RANGE : From Japan, China to Malaysian Peninsula, Myanmar, India, southern Asia.

Snake eating eggs of Common Gallinule.

Common Gallinule eggs. 1990. 7. 13.

Common Gallinule sitting on eggs among irises at lake edge. Asan Lake. 1988. 6. 6

Common Gallinule hatchlings and eggs. Asan Lake, Ch'ungch'ŏngnam Province. 1989. 6. 29.

Young Common Gallinule. P'aldang, Kyŏnggi Province. 1991. 8. 23.

Male Watercock. Ch'ŏrwon, Kangwon Province. 1986. 6. 13.

Order Gruiformes/Family Rallidae

Watercock •

Gallicrex cinerea
Korean · Tŭmbugi   33cm

Sexes similar. Whole body black; white under tail; red frontal shield with small crest, base of bill, eyes; yellow bill; in winter yellow-brown body with black spotted patterns.

STATUS : Common summer visitor. Recently numbers decreasing rapidly

HABITAT : Hides at waters edge in high grass, forest, in bushes near rice fields in daytime; active in morning and evening in rice fields and on banks.

DIET : Insects, snails, rice plants, grass sprouts.

RANGE : India, Sumatra, Philippines, China, Japan.

Male Watercock in search of female on rice field dike. Kangwon Province. 1986. 6. 13.

Coot hidden in reeds. Asan Lake, Ch'ungch'ŏngnam Province. 1987. 7. 2.

Order Gruiformes/Family Rallidae

Coot •

Fulica atra
Korean · Muldak   39cm

Sexes similar. Black body; white frontal shield and bill; red eyes; green legs; narrow white edge on secondaries; large toes
STATUS : Common transient; some breed in central areas, some winter in south.
HABITAT : Mixes with groups of ducks on lakes near reeds and water plants, in reservoirs, marshes; builds nests by piling reeds higher than Common Gallinule.
DIET : Young leaves of Graminaceae, small fish, insects, blowfish.
RANGE : All parts of Eurasia, Amur, Sakhalin, Japan.

Oystercatchers mating. Kyŏnggi Province. 1994. 6. 3.

Order Charadriiformes/Family Haematopdidae

Oystercatcher

Haematopus ostralegus
Korean · Kŏmŭnmŏrimultesae
45cm

Sexes similar. Black head, breast, back; white belly, shoulders, wing bar visible in flight; base of tail white with black bar at tip; orange bill; red eyes, legs and feet.
STATUS : Rare resident.
HABITAT : On reefs near uninhabited islands, mud banks of inlets. Winters on mud banks, estuaries, on reclaimed land in groups of 4 to 5 birds.
DIET : Molluscs, crabs, small fish.
RANGE : East coast of Kamchatka Peninsula, northern tip of Okhotsk Sea.
■ Natural Treasure No. 326.

◄ Coot. Asan Lake, Ch'ungch'ŏngnam Province. 1987. 7. 2.

Oystercatcher on rock. Ch'ŏngch'o Lake, Kangwon Province. 1994. 8. 2.

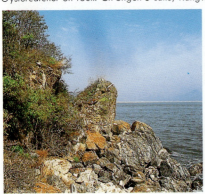
Oystercatcher breeding area. Kanghwa Island.

Oystercatcher eggs. 1992. 5. 23.

Oystercatcher at rest. Kanghwa Island. 1994. 8. 2.

Oystercatchers mating. Kanghwa Island. 1986. 4. 20.

Little Ringed Plover in search of food. Yŏngil Bay, Kyŏngsangbuk Province. 1992. 6. 14.

Order Charadriiformes/Family Charadriidae

Little Ringed Plover ●

Charadrius dubius
Korean · Komamultesae   16cm

Little Ringed Plover eggs. 1976. 8. 3.

Sexes similar. Back of head and back dark brown; white under chin, breast, belly; black line around eyes, across forehead and breast; brown legs; yellow ring around eyes.

STATUS : Common summer visitor throughout country.

HABITAT : Stream sides, rivers and streams, rice fields; well camouflaged.

DIET : Insects.

RANGE : Eurasia, from Europe to Japan, northern Africa, Mongolia, northern China.

Little Ringed Plover three day atter hatchling. Bam Island, Han River. 1988. 8. 3.

Little Ringed Plover ; note camouflage. Yangsuri, Kyŏnggi Province. 1990. 6. 15.

Little Ringed Plover at rest on rock at the edge of stream. Kyŏnggi Province. 1988. 7. 5.

Rare Long-billed Ringed Plover during migration. Sokch'o, Kangwon Province. 1972. 10. 20.

Order Charadriiformes/Family Charadriidae

Long-billed Ringed Plover •

Charadrius placidus
Korean • Hinmokmultesae 20.5cm

Sexes similar. Top of head and back, tail, wings gray-brown; wing edges black; white under chin, forehead, neck, breast, belly; black line from front of eyes to back of head; black ring around neck, thin in center.
STATUS : Uncommon transient and winter vistor.
HABITAT : Some winter over in south central area on riverside gravel, streams, lake swamps, rice fields, reclaimed land, estuaries, on coasts in groups of 3 to 5 or 15 to 20 birds.
DIET : Mainly insects.
RANGE : Temperate zone of eastern area.

Kentish Plover in summer plumage.

Kentish Plover at rest. 1987. 6. 18.

Order Charadriiformes/Family Charadriidae

Kentish Plover •

Charadrius alexandrinus
Korean · Hinmultesae   17.5cm

Male : back of head rufous ; back gray brown ; forehead, eyebrow stripes, under chin, breast, belly white ; upper forehead, beside eyes, both sides of neck black. Female : back of head brown ; upper forehead beside eyes, both sides of neck brown.

STATUS : Common transient.
HABITAT : Some winter in south in gravel areas along coast ; in rivers, estuaries, salt marshes in groups of several hundred mixed with other plovers.
DIET : Mainly insects.
RANGE : Temperate zone in eastern Siberia, Ussuri, Manchuria, northern China, Japan.

Mother Kentish Plover protecting baby. Kanghwa-gun, Kyŏnggi Province. 1987. 6. 18.

Flock of Kentish Plovers resting during migration. Kyŏnggi Province. 1989. 10. 11.

Order Charadriiformes/Family Charadriidae

Mongolian Plover ●

Charadrius mongolus
Korean • Wangnunmultesae
19.5cm

Sexes similar. Summer: top of head and back gray-brown; under chin and belly white; around eyes black; breast and side of neck red; in winter becomes gray-brown.

STATUS: Common transient in spring and autumn.

HABITAT: Sandy areas along coasts, on mudflats, in estuaries and salt marshes in groups of several tens of birds.

DIET: Insects, worms, small crabs, seeds.

RANGE: Central Siberia, eastern Arctic.

Mongolian Plover in winter plumage. Yangdari, Sokch'o, Kangwon Province. 1982. 10. 6.

Mongolian Plover in summer plumage. Yŏngil Bay, Kyŏngsangbuk Province. 1992. 6. 1.

Male Mongolian Plover. Ch'ŏngch'o Lake, Sokch'o, Kangwon Province. 1982. 5. 28.

Lesser Golden Plover in winter plumage. Sokch'o, Kangwon Province. 1988. 10. 10.

Order Charadriiformes/Family Charadriidae

Lesser Golden Plover •

Pluvialis dominica
Korean · Kŏmŭngasŭmmultesae
24cm

Sexes similar. Summer: back of head and back yellow-brown with black spots; black under chin, breast, belly; yellow-brown in winter; white band between yellow-brown and black.
STATUS : Common transient.
HABITAT : Rice fields, coastal areas, reclaimed land, salt marshes, estuaries in groups of 2 or 3 or several hundred; flies in 'V' formation.
DIET : Insects, worms, shellfish, seeds, berries.

Lesser Golden Plover resting. 1988. 10. 10.

RANGE : All of northern area, Arctic tundra from Siberia to Arctic area of North America.

Black-bellied Plover in winter plumage. Ch'ŏngch'o Lake, Kangwon Province. 1988. 10. 10.

Order Charadriiformes / Family Charadriidae

Black-bellied Plover ●

Pluvialis squatarola
Korean · Kaekwŏng   29.5cm

Sexes similar. Grayish white head; back mottled black; white forehead, shoulders, under tail; black under chin, breast, belly; becomes grayish white in winter.
STATUS : Common transient.

HABITAT : Reclaimed land along coast, estuaries, marshes in groups mixed with sandpipers of up to several hundred; searches for food on tidal land; flies in straight line or in 'V' formation; very small number winter in southern area.
DIET : Worms, shrimp, shellfish, insects, seeds.
RANGE : Whole northern area, Arctic tundra, from northern Russia to Siberia, Alaska, Arctic area of North America.

Lapwing in winter. Ch'ŏngch'o Lake, Sokch'o, Kangwon Province. 1982. 2. 14.

Order Charadriiformes/Family Charadriidae

Lapwing •

Vanellus vanellus
Korean • Taenggimultesae 31.5cm

Sexes similar. Black plume on head, pattern on cheeks, breast, under chin; belly, white; red feet; brownish yellow-green back, wings.

STATUS : Common winter visitor, passes through Korea on spring and autumn migrations.
HABITAT : South central areas; rice fields, dry fields, marshes, riversides, reclaimed land in estuaries in groups of 3 or 4 to several hundred.
DIET : Insects, worms, seeds.
RANGE : Temperate zone, Arctic, grasslands, deserts.

Lapwing in search of food along coast. Sokch'o, Kangwon Province. 1983. 2. 14.

Lapwing flock in winter. Ch'ŏngch'o Lake, Sokch'o, Kangwon Province. 1983. 1. 2.

Ruddy Turnstone in winter plumage. Ch'ŏngch'o Lake, Kangwon Province. 1987. 10. 5.

Order Charadriiformes/Family Scolopacidae

Ruddy Turnstone ●

Arenaria interpres
Korean · Kokadoyo   22cm

Male : red brown back with black stripes, white head. Female : dark brown back, head; black stripes on cheeks, breast; white belly; red legs.
STATUS : Common transient.
HABITAT : Rocky areas, coastal beaches, estuaries; in groups of 2 or 3 to several tens.
DIET : small shrimp, fish, shellfish, worms.
RANGE : Arctic areas.

Young Ruddy Turnstone. Ch'ŏngch'o Lake, Sokch'o, Kangwon Province. 1987. 10. 5.

Ruddy Turnstones in search of food. Yŏngil-gun, Kyŏngsangbuk Province. 1988. 6. 3.

Rufous-necked Stint in winter plumage in search of food. Kyŏnggi Province. 1983. 10. 3.

Order Charadriiformes/Family Scolopacidae

Rufous-necked Stint •

Calidris ruficollis
Korean • Chomdoyo   15cm

Sexes similar. Summer: rufous head and upper breast. Winter: gray-brown pattern on back and wings; white lower breast and belly; black feet and bill.
STATUS : Common transient.
HABITAT : Reclaimed land along coasts, in marshes, grassy swamps near coast, reclaimed land in estuaries, salt marshes in groups of 5 or 6 to several tens of birds mixed with Dunlin.
DIET : Shellfish, worms, insects.
RANGE : Eastern Siberian tundra, coast of Okhotsk Sea, eastern China, Japan.

Rufous-necked Stints in summer plumage. P'ohang, Kyŏngsangbuk Province. 1992. 6. 3.

Long-toed Stint in search of food. Hwajŏn, Koyang-gun, Kyŏnggi Province. 1992. 6. 6.

Order Charadriiformes/Family Scolopacidae

Long-toed Stint ●

Calidris minutilla
Korean · Chongdaldoyo 14.5cm

Sexes similar. Brown head, breast, back with black and dark brown pattern ; rufous on wings ; white lower breast, belly and face ; yellowish green legs.
STATUS : Transient.
HABITAT : In spring and autumn : Inch'ŏn, Chogandae near southern coast, Miruji in Kanghwa Island, rice fields in Hwajŏn in Kyŏnggi Province in May, September and October.
DIET : Small shellfish, fish, spiders, insects, seeds.
RANGE : Eastern Siberia.

Sharp-tailed Sandpiper in search of food. Kanghwa-gun, Kyŏnggi Province. 1988. 6. 11.

Order Charadriiformes/Family Scolopacidae

Sharp-tailed Sandpiper ●

Calidris acuminata
Korean · Mechuragidoyo 21.5cm

Sexes similar. Crown rufous; back brown; white belly with black pattern; brown breast and sides; black wing edge; white edges on tail.
STATUS : Common transient
HABITAT : Reclaimed land along coasts, salt marshes, estuaries, rice fields; alone or in groups of 2 to 4 birds.
DIET : Shellfish, insects, worms.
RANGE : Tundra of eastern Siberia, Kamchatka Peninsula, Sakhalin, Taiwan.

Dunlin in winter plumage. Ŭlsuk Island, Naktong River. 1983. 1. 6.

Order Charadriiformes/Family Scolopacidae

Dunlin •

Calidris alpina
Korean • Minmuldoyo   21cm

Sexes similar. Summer : black on belly ; rufous with black and brown pattern on back. Winter : gray-brown over almost all of body ; white belly ; black bill and legs.

STATUS : Common transient, most numerous shorebird visiting Korea.

HABITAT : Winters on southern coast, islands ; reclaimed land, coastal grassland, salt marshes.

DIET : Shellfish, snails, worms, spiders, insects.

RANGE : Northeastern Siberia, southern Okhotsk Sea, eastern China, Japan.

Flock of Dunlins. Ŭlsuk Island, Naktong River. 1987. 2. 3.

Dunlins in search of food. Sorae, Shihŭng-gun, Kyŏnggi Province. 1988. 10. 3.

Curlew Sandpiper at rest. Sorae, Shihŭng-gun, Kyŏnggi Province. 1982. 10. 18.

Order Charadriiformes/Family Scolopacidae

Curlew Sandpiper •

Calidris ferruginea
Korean • Pulgŭngaettoyo 21.5cm

Sexes similar. Summer: rufous with black, white and gray pattern on whole of body. Winter: gray-brown head, back; white eye stripe, breast, belly.
STATUS : Transient.
HABITAT : Along west coast in small groups in spring and autumn; reclaimed land, marshes, estuaries, salt marshes.
DIET : Worms, shellfish, insects.
RANGE : Eastern Siberian tundra.

Great Knots at rest on coast during migration. Sŏngsanp'o, Cheju Island. 1992. 6. 14.

Order Charadriiformes/Family Scolopacidae

Great Knot •

Calidris tenuirostris
Korean · Pulgŭnŏkaedoyo 28.5cm

Sexes similar. Summer : white head with brown pattern ; breast black-brown with white pattern becoming brown in winter ; back dark gray with red pattern ; white under chin ; white eye stripe and belly.
STATUS : Common transient.
HABITAT : Reclaimed land along coast and in estuaries, salt marshes ; in groups of 4~5 to several thousand.
DIET : Shellfish, snails, worms, insects.
RANGE : Arctic area of northeastern Siberia, coast of Okhotsk Sea, Alaska, Japan, Taiwan.

Great Knot at rest along the coast. Ullŭng Island. 1989. 4. 18.

Sanderling in search of food on seashore. Ülsuk Island, Naktong River. 1986. 2. 6.

Order Charadriiformes/Family Scolopacidae

Sanderling ●

Crocethia alba
Korean · Segaraktoyo   19cm

Sexes similar. Rufous head, breast, with black and gray pattern on back. Winter: gray head, back; black shoulders, wing edges; white under chin, belly, and breast.

STATUS : Transient.

HABITAT : Winters in south along coast, reclaimed land, beaches and estuaries in groups of 2 or 3 to several hundred mixed with Dunlin and Rufous-necked Stints.

DIET : Shellfish, worms, insects, small fish.

RANGE : Tundra of Arctic Siberia, Arctic islands of North America, Philippines, Australia, Sakhalin, Japan.

Sanderlings in search of food in river estuary. Ayajin, Kangwon Province. 1990. 10. 23.

Broad-billed Sandpiper at rest on estuary mudflat. Sorae, Kyŏnggi Province. 1976. 10. 3.

Order Charadriiformes/Family Scolopacidae

Broad-billed Sandpiper •

Limicola falcinellus
Korean • Songgotpuridoyo   17cm

Sexes similar. Summer: black crown stripes; brown breast; white belly back with rufous pattern. Winter: light gray head, back.
STATUS : Transient.
HABITAT : Reclaimed land along coasts, shallow water, marshes, reclaimed land in estuaries, salt marshes; alone or in groups of 2 to 5 mixed with Rufous-necked Stint or Dunlin.
DIET : Insects, worms, shellfish, seeds.
RANGE : Siberia, Mediterranean Sea, western India, South Asia.

Spotted Redshank in search of food in reservoir. Miruji, Kyŏnggi Province. 1988. 10. 1.

Order Charadriiformes/Family Scolopacidae

Spotted Redshank •

Tringa erythropus
Korean · Haktoyo　　　　　32.5cm

Sexes similar. Summer: all black with gray pattern. Winter: dark gray back; rest gray-white; base of bill, legs red.

STATUS : Comparatively common transient.
HABITAT : Reclaimed land along coasts, in shallow water, marshes, reeds along rivers and streams, reclaimed land in estuaries, rice fields, ponds in groups of 30 to 40 and up to 250 to 300; fly in irregular lines.
DIET : Insects, shellfish, frogs, tadpoles, small shrimp.
RANGE : Eastern Siberia, Africa, Sakhalin, Japan.

Spotted Redshank on the wing. Miruji, Kanghwa-gun, Kyŏnggi Province. 1988. 10. 1.

Spotted Redshank at rest. Miruji, Kanghwa-gun Kyŏnggi Province. 1988. 10. 2.

Spotted Redshanks in search of food on estuary mudflat. 1988. 10. 2.

Redshank in search of food. Kimp'o, Kyŏnggi Province. 1987. 10. 3.

Order Charadriiformes/Family Scolopacidae

Redshank ●

Tringa totanus
Korean · Pulgŭnbaldoyo   27.5cm

Sexes similar. Summer : brown head ; back dark brown pattern ; white breast and belly with brown streaks. Winter : light brown head, shoulders, back ; base of bill, legs red.
STATUS : Uncommon transient.
HABITAT : Marshes along coasts, reclaimed land, salt marshes, swamps in bay areas, reclaimed land in estuaries, small ponds ; walk or swim in water submerged to the depth of breast.
DIET : Insects, shellfish, worms.
RANGE : Central and eastern Asia, Amur River, Himalayas, northern Japan ; winters in India, Myanmar, Philippines.

Marsh Sandpipers in search of food. Chongdalri, Sŏngsan, Cheju Island. 1992. 4. 13.

Order Charadriiformes/Family Scolopacidae

Marsh Sandpiper ●

Tringa stagnatilis
Korean · Soechŏngdaridoyo
24.5cm

Sexes similar. White eye stripe, cheeks, throat, breast, belly, flanks, tail; 5~6 gray-brown stripes on tail; dark gray mottled back, head; edge of wing black; thin black bill thinner than Greenshank's.
STATUS : Rare transient.
HABITAT : Marshes along coasts, beside ponds, on estuaries, reedy areas alone or in groups of 4 or 5.
DIET : Insects, shellfish, worms.
RANGE : Northern Caspian Sea, Black Sea, valley of Amur River; winters in Africa, India, Australia.

Greenshank in winter plumage. Inch'ŏn coastal area, Kyŏnggi Province. 1981. 10. 10.

Order Charadriiformes/Family Scolopacidae

Greenshank •

Tringa nebularia
Korean · Chŏngdaridoyo   35cm

Sexes similar. Summer: white head, breast, shoulders with dark gray pattern; white breast, shoulders. Winter: pale gray back; white belly, flanks, tail; greenish gray legs.
STATUS : Common transient.
HABITAT : Reclaimed land along coasts, estuaries, salt marshes, inland rivers and streams, ponds, reservoirs in groups of 2 or 3 to 20 ~50 birds; fly in a line.
DIET : Insects, shellfish, tadpoles, small fish.
RANGE : Tundra areas.

Greenshanks at rest during migration. Ch'ungch'ŏngnam Province. 1982. 9. 20.

Greenshank at rest on estuary mudflat. Sorae, Shihŭng-gun, Kyŏnggi Province. 1984. 10. 10.

Male and female Wood Sandpiper in search of food. Kyŏnggi Province. 1992. 6. 6.

Order Charadriiformes/Family Scolopacidae

Wood Sandpiper •

Tringa glareola
Korean • Allaktoyo   21.5cm

Sexes similar. Dark gray brown top of head, back of neck, eye stripe, back and wings with many white spots; white cheeks, breast, belly, tail with dark brown streaks except on belly.
STATUS : Common transient.
HABITAT : Beside rivers, estuaries, streams, rice fields and swamps in groups of 5 or 6 or less.
DIET : Insects, spiders, small shellfish.
RANGE : From Siberian tundra through parts of temperate zone.

Wood Sandpiper in search of food.

Gray-tailed Tattler eating small crabs on coast. Kyŏngsangbuk Province. 1992. 5. 29.

Order Charadriiformes/Family Scolopacidae

Gray-tailed Tattler ●

Tringa brevipes
Korean · Norangbaldoyo   25cm

Sexes similar. Dark gray on back of head and back; black wing edges; white eye stripe, cheeks, breast, belly; dark brown stripes on breast; yellow legs.

STATUS : Common transient.

HABITAT : Reclaimed land along coasts; reefs with seaweed attached; bays, beaches, inlet mud, estuaries, salt marshes; alone or in groups; walks very fast with tail moving up and down; flies in groups in single file.

DIET : Shellfish, insects, small fish.

RANGE : Eastern Siberia.

Gray-tailed Tattlers at rest along coast. P'ohang, Kyŏngsangbuk Province. 1992. 5. 29.

Common Sandpiper in summer. Apkokri, Hoengsŏng-gun, Kangwon Province. 1992. 8. 11.

Order Charadriiformes/Family Scolopacidae

Common Sandpiper ●

Tringa hypoleucos
Korean · Kapchaktoyo   20cm

Common Sandpiper eggs. 1984. 5. 5.

Sexes similar. Dark brown on top of head, back of neck, wings; white stripe on wings; white eye stripe, under chin, cheeks, shoulders, breast, belly; brown on cheeks and breast.
STATUS: Summer visitor.
HABITAT: Reefs along coasts, inland streams, rivers, brooks; walks bobbing head and tail; builds nest on sand or gravel or in spaces between roots of trees.
DIET: Insects, shellfish, shrimp, spiders.
RANGE: From Siberian temperate zone to Arctic, from Europe to Siberia, Mongolia, China, Japan.

Terek Sandpiper in search of food during migration. Kangwon Province. 1985. 10. 5.

Order Charadriiformes/Family Scolopacidae

Terek Sandpiper •

Xenus cinereus
Korean • Twitpuridoyo   23cm

Sexes similar. Summer: top of head, beside eyes, back, gray; black lines on back; eyebrow, under chin, belly white; brown breast; black, upturned bill with yellow base. Winter: top of head, eye stripe, back gray-brown; rest becomes paler than in summer.
STATUS : Rare transient.
HABITAT : Reclaimed land along coast, estuaries, mudflats, salt marshes in groups of 2 or 3 mixed with Dunlin and Gray-tailed Tattlers; calls on the wing when in search of food.
DIET : Mainly insects.
RANGE : Northern Europe to Siberia.

◄ Common Sandpiper at rest in reeds beside river. Tŭkso, Kyŏnggi Province. 1987. 7. 20.

Flock of Terek Sandpipers in search of food. Ülsuk Island, Naktong River. 1986. 10. 5.

Black-tailed Godwit in winter plumage. Sorae, Kyŏnggi Province. 1976. 10. 4.

Order Charadriiformes/Family Scolopacidae

Black-tailed Godwit •

Limosa limosa
Korean · Hŭkkoridoyo   38.5cm

Sexes similar. Summer: red head, breast; dark gray with black and red patterns on back. Winter: gray-brown head, back; white breast, belly, tail base; black band on tip of tail; tip of bill black; orange base of bill.
STATUS: Common transient.
HABITAT: Reclaimed land along coast, marshes, salt marshes and estuaries, rice fields; in groups of 2 to 10 or 200 to 300 mixed with Bar-tailed Godwits; flies in groups in line.
DIET: Insects, spiders, snails, worms, tadpoles, shellfish.
RANGE: From Kamchatka Peninsula to eastern Siberia.

Black-tailed Godwits preening. Sorae, Shihŭng-gun, Kyŏnggi Province. 1983. 9. 28.

Black-tailed Godwits in search of food. Haengjusansŏng, Han River, Seoul. 1984. 6. 6.

Bar-tailed Godwit in search of food on estuary mudflats. Kyŏnggi Province. 1991. 9. 17.

Order Charadriiformes/Family Scolopacidae

Bar-tailed Godwit •

Limosa lapponica
Korean · Kŭntwitpuridoyo   41cm

Sexes similar. Summer: red head, breast, belly; blackish back. Winter: grayish white with brown pattern on belly; tip of bill black, upturned bill with flesh colored base.

STATUS: Common transient.

HABITAT: Reclaimed land along coast, swamps, bays, estuaries, salt marshes; 2 to 3 or several hundred birds mixed with Black-tailed Godwits, Black-bellied Plover, Lesser Golden Plover; fly in line and come down after circling two or three times.

DIET: Shellfish, invertebrates, polychaeta.

RANGE: From eastern Siberia to the coast of northwestern Alaska.

Bar-tailed Godwit at rest. Miruji, Kanghwa-gun, Kyŏnggi Province. 1987. 10. 8.

Bar-tailed Godwits in search of food. Cheju Island. 1994. 1. 6.

Australian Curlew eating crabs on estuary mudflats. Cheju Island. 1992. 10. 20.

Order Charadriiformes/Family Scolopacidae

Australian Curlew •

Numenius madagascariensis
Korean • Allakkorimadoyo 61.5cm

Australian Curlew at rest.

Sexes similar. Brown with dark brown and black stripes over whole body; bluish gray legs; white under chin; brown, strongly down-curved bill.
STATUS : Common transient.
HABITAT : Winters in south; coastal mudflats, reclaimed land in estuaries, salt marshes, tilled fields; alone or in groups of several hundred mixed with other curlews.
DIET : shellfish, shrimp, insects, invertebrates, small fish; plants during breeding season.
RANGE : Coast of Okhotsk Sea, Ussuri, Philippines, Australia, Sakhalin, Japan, Taiwan.

Australian Curlew in search of food on estuary mudflat. Kyŏnggi Province. 1984. 10. 8.

Whimbrel eating crab. Sorae, Shihŭng-gun, Kyŏnggi Province. 1987. 9. 13.

Order Charadriiformes/Family Scolopacidae

Whimbrel ●

Numenius phaeopus
Korean · Chungburidoyo   41cm

Sexes similar. Dark brown crown stripe; brown with gray spots on back; light brown with dark brown stripes on cheeks, breast, belly; down curved bill.

STATUS: Transient; more pass through in spring than in autumn.

HABITAT: Dry fields inland, on coast in estuaries, salt marshes, tilled fields, marshes, swamps; alone or in groups of several tens of birds mixed with other kinds of shorebirds.

DIET: Shellfish, shrimp, insects, worms, small fish.

RANGE: Tundra, Arctic regions, mountainous areas, eastern Siberia, Australia.

Whimbrel in search of food on coast of Inch'ŏn Harbor. Kyŏnggi Province. 1983. 9. 20.

Whimbrel in winter plumage on coast of Inch'ŏn Harbor. Kyŏnggi Province. 1983. 9. 20.

Whimbrels in search of food. Taesong Island, Kanghwa-gun, Kyŏnggi Province. 1992. 5. 5.

Common Snipe in search of food. Hwajŏn, Koyang-gun, Kyŏnggi Province. 1992. 5. 30.

Order Charadriiformes/Family Scolopacidae

Common Snipe ●

Gallinago gallinago
Korean · Kaktoyo   27cm

Sexes similar. Light yellow-brown with brown streaks, on head and breast; dark brown stripe under and above eyes; grayish white with brown stripes on belly; rufous with yellowish brown pattern on back; red band on tail.
STATUS: Common transient.
HABITAT: Some winter in south central area along coast in reed beds, grassland near swamps, reclaimed land, rice fields, estuary shores; in flocks during migration; scatter in small groups of 2 or 3 birds when in danger.
DIET: Worms, spiders, insects, shellfish, snails, loach, seeds.
RANGE: Scandinavia to eastern Siberia, Sakhalin.

Common Snipe at rest in rice field. Hwajŏn, Koyang-gun, Kyŏnggi Province. 1992. 5. 30.

Black-winged Stilt at rest. Hadori nursery on Cheju Island. 1992. 6. 18.

Order Charadriiformes/Family Recurvirostridae

Black-winged Stilt ○

Himantopus himantopus
Korean · Changdarimultesae 31cm

Male: greenish black head, back, back of neck, wings; white cheeks, neck, breast, belly.
Female: white head, neck; black bill; exceptionally long red legs.
STATUS : Very rare stray recorded in Chinch'ŏn, Ch'ungch'ŏngbuk Province, Changja Island, Naktong River estuary; latest record and picture, Hadori, Cheju Island.
HABITAT : Walk quietly looking for food in shallow sea or fresh water, bob when they stop.
DIET : Frogs, tadpoles, lizards, insects, small fish, shellfish.
RANGE : Whole world from temperate zone to the tropics.

Black-winged Stilts in search of food. Hadori, Cheju Island. 1992. 6. 18.

Black-winged Stilts at rest in reservoir along coast. Hadori, Cheju Island. 1992. 6. 16.

Northern Phalaropes at rest on estuary mudflats near coast. Chŏllanam Province. 1980. 8. 26.

Order Charadriiformes/Family Phalaropodidae

Northern Phalarope ●

Phalaropus lobatus
Korean · Chinŭrŏmibaldoyo 19cm

Summer: top of head and back black; reddish upper breast to ear; female redder than male with red on back. Winter: top of head and around eyes black; white cheeks, breast; gray back.
STATUS : Transient passing along southern and eastern coasts in spring and autumn.
HABITAT : Salt marshes along coast or on sea often in groups of hundreds; feeds while swimming in a zigzag pattern.
DIET : Water insects.
RANGE : Arctic coasts, fresh water inland, northern Siberia, coast of Okhotsk Sea, northern Alaska, North America.

Indian Pratincole at rest. Haengjusansŏng, Han River, Seoul. 1981. 10. 3.

Order Charadriiformes/Family Glareolidae

Indian Pratincole ●

Glareola maldivarum
Korean · Chebimultesae 26.5cm

Sexes similar. Summer: red at base of bill, inside of wings; black tip of wings, feet, line from eyes to breast, but fades in winter; light yellow under chin; changes to same yellowish brown as whole body in winter; white belly.

STATUS : Transient; passes in small groups.

HABITAT : Reclaimed land along coasts, swamps, estuaries, mudflats, sandy shores, dry fields.

DIET : Insects, dragonflies, worms.

RANGE : Temperate zone of Asia and tropics.

Young Indian Pratincole at rest beside river during migration. Han River, Seoul. 1987. 9. 4.

Black-headed Gull in winter preening. Ŭlsuk Island, Naktong River. 1986. 8. 29.

Order Charadriiformes/Family Laridae

Black-headed Gull •

Larus ridibundus
Korean • Pulgŭnburigalmaegi
40cm

Sexes similar. Brownish black head; become white except spots on head in winter; red bill, legs; gray back, wings with white leading edge, black tip; white body, tail.

STATUS : Common winter visitor.
HABITAT : Along east and south sea coasts; usually floating on surface of sea; sits on reefs, banks, buildings, tree branches; at rest faces into wind standing on one leg; less common on west coast.
DIET : Fish, insects, spiders, shellfish, pieces of fish, food remains.
RANGE : Eastern Siberia, Kamchatka Peninsula, Sakhalin; winters in Korea, China, Japan.

Black-headed Gull in summer. 1986. 8. 29.

Black-headed Gulls at rest on beach. P'ohang, Kyŏngsangbuk Province. 1989. 10. 5. ▶

Herring Gulls in coastal reservoir. Miruji, Kyŏnggi Province. 1989. 11. 2.

Order Charadriiformes/Family Laridae

Herring Gull •

Larus argentatus
Korean · Chaegalmaegi 60cm

Sexes similar. Yellow bill with red spot on gonys; gray wings; black tip of wings with white spot; rest white; brown pattern from head to breast in winter.
STATUS : Common winter visitor.
HABITAT : Sandy areas along coast, islands, reclaimed land in estuaries in flocks of 100 to 200 birds mixed with Black-tailed Gulls; sometimes groups of 20 to 50 Herring Gulls only; flies in columnar groups at regular intervals when in search of food.
DIET : Dead bodies of animals and birds, fish, shellfish, insects, plants.
RANGE : Coast of northern Siberia, northern Okhotsk Sea.

Young Herring Gull in search of food under Chungrang Bridge, Seoul. 1986. 11. 6.

Herring Gulls at rest in reservoir. Miruji, Kanghwa-gun, Kyŏnggi Province. 1989. 11. 2.

Slaty-backed Gull in winter. Ch'ŏngch'o Lake, Kangwon Province. 1992. 1. 20.

Order Charadriiformes/Family Laridae

Slaty-backed Gull •

Larus schistisagus
Korean · Kŭnjaegalmaegi   61cm

Sexes similar. Yellow bill with red spot near gonys; dark gray-black wings with black and white spots on edges; rest white, acquiring a brown pattern on cheeks and neck in winter; legs reddish pink.
STATUS : Comparatively rare winter visitor.
HABITAT : Coasts, reefs, estuaries small groups of Slaty-backed Gulls with Black-tailed Gulls and Herring Gulls winter together; when flying moves head side to side and holds feet against belly.
DIET : Dead animals and birds, fish intestines, shellfish, Annelidae, insects.
RANGE : North Pacific Ocean, coast of Okhotsk Sea, Kamchatka Peninsula, Kuril Archipelago, Sakhalin, Hokkaido.

Young Slaty-backed Gull. Ayajin, Kosŏng-gun, Kangwon Province. 1987. 12. 29.

Slaty-backed Gulls along coast. Chumunjin, Kangwon Province. 1987. 12. 28.

Black-tailed Gull in winter. Ch'ŏngch'o Lake, Sokch'o, Kangwon Province. 1987. 12. 20.

Order Charadriiformes/Family Laridae

Black-tailed Gull

Larus crassirostris
Korean · Koengigalmaegi   46.5cm

Sexes similar. Yellow bill and legs ; red and black band on tip of bill ; black line end of tail ; dark gray wings, back ; black wing tips ; rest white.
STATUS : Common resident.
HABITAT : All coasts, islands, reefs, estuaries in groups in search of food ; build nests in large colonies on islands offshore.
DIET : Fish, amphibia, shellfish, insects, remains of food or fish.
RANGE : Japan, southern Yŏnhaeju, coast of China, southern Sakhalin, southern Kuril Archipelago.

The largest Black-tailed Gull breeding area in Korea. 1989. 6. 3. (p.p. 254~255)

Black-tailed Gull eggs. 1990. 6. 6.

Black-tailed Gull baby and eggs.

Pair of Black-tailed Gulls courting. Hong Island, Kyŏngsangnam Province. 1990. 6. 6.

Black-tailed Gulls at rest. Naktong River, Ŭlsuk Island. 1986. 2. 7.

Black-tailed Gulls feeding nestlings. Shin Island, Ongjin-gun, Kyŏnggi Province 1991. 6. 18.

Black-legged Kittiwake in winter. Ayajin, Kosŏng-gun, Kangwon Province. 1987. 1. 21.

Order Charadriiformes / Family Laridae

Black-legged Kittiwake ●

Larus tridactylus
Korean · Segarakkalmaegi   39cm

Sexes similar. Black spot on back of head; black feet and edges of wings; gray on back, wings; yellow bill; rest white.

STATUS: Very rare winter visitor.

HABITAT: Winters in small fishing ports on eastern sea coast near 38th parallel in groups of 20 to 50 birds; seen especially around fishing ports where there are large catches of Alaskan Pollack.

DIET: Fish, shellfish, Annelidae some plants.

RANGE: Alaska, Kamchatka Peninsula, Sakhalin, Aleutian Archipelago; winters in Korea, Japan, California.

Black-legged Kittiwake asleep. 1987. 1. 21.

Black-legged Kittiwakes in winter on east coast. Ayajin, Kangwon Province. 1986. 1. 30.

Common Tern at rest during migration. Ch'ŏngch'o Lake, Kangwon Province. 1983. 10. 3.

Order Charadriiformes/Family Laridae

Common Tern •

Sterna hirundo
Korean · Chebigalmaegi   35.5cm

Sexes similar. Bill, top of head, feet, edge of wings black; in winter forehead becomes white; bluish gray back, wings; gray belly in winter becomes white.

STATUS : Comparatively common transient.
HABITAT : Lakes, coasts, estuaries; in groups when searching for food; in groups of 2 to 4 or several tens when migrating; sit on sandy beaches or marshy ground, preen on poles.
DIET : Small fish, insects.
RANGE : Eastern Siberia, Kamchatka Peninsula, Sakhalin, Kuril Archipelago; south through Korea and Japan; winter in southeast Asia.

Common Terns at rest. Ch'ŏngch'o Lake, Sokch'o, Kangwon Province. 1982. 10. 5.

Common Terns at rest. Ch'ŏngch'o Lake, Sokch'o, Kangwon Province. 1986. 10. 1.

Male and female Little Tern in breeding season. Ch'ungch'ŏngbuk Province. 1987. 8. 11.

Order Charadriiformes/Family Laridae

Little Tern ●

Sterna albifrons
Korean • Soejebigalmaegi   28cm

Sexes similar. Back of head, eye stripe, wing edges black; orange bill with black tip and feet; pale gray back, wings. Winter: black bill; white in front of eyes; white forehead, cheeks, breast, tail.
STATUS : Common summer visitor.
HABITAT : Coasts, sandy areas beside rivers, gravelly areas in groups; when flying legs held against belly; sits on ground, stakes, floating wood to preen.
DIET : Small fish.
RANGE : Japan, Siberia; winters in Philippines, New Guinea, Australia, Indo-China, India.

Little Tern eight day after hatching. Bam Island, Han River. 1986. 6. 6.

Little Tern eggs. Bam Island. 1986. 6. 6.

Little Tern at rest on rice field dike. Mi Lake, Ch'ungch'ŏngbuk Province. 1987. 8. 11. ▶

Ancient Murrelet in search of food in the sea. Chŏllanam Province. 1987. 4. 10.

Order Charadriiformes/Family Alcidae

Ancient Murrelet

Synthliboramphus antiquus
Korean · Padasoeori   25.5cm

Sexes similar. Summer: black head, throat; white pattern from behind eyes to neck; dark gray back; white belly breast, sides of neck. Winter: no white pattern behind eyes; yellow-brown bill.
STATUS: Common resident.
HABITAT: Uninhabited islands of Yellow Sea, East Sea; winters on south coast; in groups of 3 or 4, 20 or 30 to several hundred in winter, flies close to surface of sea in line; dives for food.
DIET: Small fish, shellfish.

Ancient Murrelet eggs. 1987. 4. 10.

RANGE: Coast of Okhotsk Sea, Aleutian Archipelago, southern Alaska, Amur River, Sakhalin, Japan.

Female and male Rock Dove at rest in field. Ongjin-gun, Kyŏnggi Province. 1988. 8. 8.

Order Columbiformes/Family Columbidae

Rock Dove

Columba rupestris
Korean · Yangbidulgi   32cm

Sexes similar. Dark gray head; glossy green on sides of neck; chestnut breast; gray back and wings with two black striped patterns on back; black bill; red legs.
STATUS : Resident.
HABITAT : Breeds throughout country, streams, brooks in mountains, beside lakes, rivers, on rocks, rocky cliffs, limestone caves on coast; rocky inland mountains, piers in groups of 10 to 30 birds or more.
DIET : Grain plants.
RANGE : Middle and eastern Asia, northern China, western Tibet, southern Himalayas.

◄ Ancient Murrelet on nest in breeding season. Chŏllanam Province. 1987. 4. 10.

Flock of Rock Doves on the wing. Ongjin-gun, Kyŏnggi Province. 1988. 8. 8.

Rock Doves in search of food in dry field. Ongjin-gun, Kyŏnggi Province. 1988. 8. 8.

Japanese Wood Pigeon eating Machilus fruit. Chŏllanam Province. 1990. 8. 15.

Order Columbiformes/Family Columbidae

Japanese Wood Pigeon

Columba janthina
Korean · Hŭkpidulgi   40cm

Sexes similar. Black over whole body glossed with purple, green, and red; whitish with black bill; red legs.

STATUS : Rare resident.
HABITAT : Islands in East, Yellow Sea and southern sea areas, on Machilus bushes, on branches of evergreens and broad-leafed trees, holes in trees; builds nest on rocks.
DIET : Fruit of Machilus, Phytolacca americana, plants.
RANGE : Southern Japan, China.
■ Natural Treasure No. 215.

Rufous Turtle Dove seen commonly in dry fields. Kyŏnggi Province. 1980. 6. 6.

Order Columbiformes/Family Columbidae

Rufous Turtle Dove

Streptopelia orientalis
Korean · Metpidulgi   33cm

Sexes similar. Pinkish gray head, breast, belly; 4 or 5 black horizontal stripes on sides of neck; rufous and black patterns on back and scapular; grayish in center of wing; black wing tip, tail.
STATUS : Common resident seen everywhere.
HABITAT : In pairs in summer, in small groups in winter; in bushes and grassy fields.
DIET : Grain, seeds and fruits, beans, green pepper seeds.
RANGE : Southern Siberia, Sakhalin, Japan, China, Himalayas.

◀ Japanese Wood Pigeon in Machilus bush. Chŏllanam Province. 1990. 8. 16.

Rufous Turtle Dove in search of food in grassy field. Ch'ungch'ŏngbuk Province. 1992. 5. 20.

Rufous Turtle Dove on eggs. 1980. 6. 6.

Rufous Turtle Dove with two eggs. 1980. 6. 6.

Male and female Rufous Turtle Dove at rest in a tree. Chunam Reservoir. 1992. 2. 15.

Female Common Cuckoo. Pǔphǔng Temple, Kangwon Province. 1992. 8. 15.

Order Cuculiformes/Family Culculidae

Common Cuckoo •

Cuculus canorus
Korean • Pŏkkugi   35cm

Sexes similar. Gray head, breast, back; edge of wings, tail black; many spots in striped patterns on tail; white belly with narrow black stripes; yellow legs.
STATUS: Common summer visitor.
HABITAT: Alone in forest; lays eggs in other birds' nests; young raised by other birds.
DIET: Insect larvae, eggs.

Common Cuckoo on the wing. 1989. 6. 10.

RANGE: Eastern Siberia, Kuril Archipelago, Japan.

Common Cuckoo near another bird's nest. Yangsuri, Kyŏnggi Province. 1989. 7. 20.

Solitary Little Cuckoo living in a village. Munsan, P'aiu-gun, Kyŏnggi Province. 1987. 8. 2.

Order Cuculiformes/Family Cuculidae

Little Cuckoo ●

Cuculus poliocephalus
Korean · Tugyŏni   27.5cm

Sexes similar. Dark gray head, breast, back, wings; black with white bars on wing edges and tail; white belly with large black stripes, bigger than those of Common Cuckoo.
STATUS : Summer visitor.
HABITAT : Commonly sits alone on tree branch in tilled area; lays eggs in other birds nests; usually in Bush Warbler's nests and they raise the young.
DIET : Imago, larvae, insect, eggs.
RANGE : Ussuri, Manchuria, southwestern China, Himalayas, India, Kenya, Japan.

Little Cuckoo preening. Munsan, P'aiu-gun, Kyŏnggi Province. 1987. 8. 2. ▶

Eagle Owl. Naech'on-myŏn, P'och'ŏn-gun, Kyŏnggi Province. 1992. 6. 2.

Order Strigiformes/Family Strigidae

Eagle Owl

Bubo bubo
Korean · Suribuŏngi   66cm

Sexes similar. Whole body yellowish brown; vertical pattern of black spots on breast, back, wings; dark brown patterns on rest of body; two big black 'ears' on head.
STATUS : Comparatively rare resident.
HABITAT : Cliffs, rocky mountains in isolated areas and cliffs in northern parts of central area; active at night; breeds on rocky cliffs, shelves or in spaces between rocks and in rocky caves.
DIET : Pheasants, hares, rats, frogs, snakes, lizards, insects.
RANGE : Eastern China.
■ Natural Treasure No. 324.

Eagle Owls eight day after hatching. P'och'ŏn-gun, Kyŏnggi Province. 1992. 5. 17.

Eagle Owl excrement. 1992. 5. 17.

Eagle Owl breeding habitat. 1992. 5. 17.

Eagle Owl protecting young birds in nearby nest. Kyŏnggi Province. 1992. 6. 2.

Eagle Owls sixteen day after hatching. Kyŏnggi Province. 1992. 6. 2.

Long-eared Owl on Kyŏnghee University campus in winter. Seoul. 1981. 1. 23.

Order Strigiformes/Family Strigidae

Long-eared Owl •

Asio otus
Korean · Chikpuŏngi   38cm

Sexes similar. Light grayish yellow-brown over whole body; vertical lines of brown spots on breast, belly, tail; spotted dark brown on back, wings; large ear tufts.
STATUS : Winter visitor. Number is decreasing.
HABITAT : Likes narrow leafed trees such as pines; active at night; uses old nests of Common Buzzard or Falcon in mixed woods or in roots of tall trees.
DIET : Field rats, moles, small birds.
RANGE : Arctic and temperate areas.
■ Natural Treasure No. 324.

Short-eared Owl in search of food. Nanjido, Han River, Seoul. 1982. 2. 7.

Order Strigiformes/Family Strigidae

Short-eared Owl ●

Asio flammeus
Korean · Soebuŏngi　　38.5cm

Sexes similar. Tawny over whole body; black striped pattern on back of wings; dark brown streaks on breast, belly; small ear tufts.
STATUS : Winter visitor.
HABITAT : Grassy-shrubby areas; reed fields, reclaimed land, trees in reclaimed areas.
DIET : Field rats, insects, small wild birds.
RANGE : Arctic, temperate zones, Siberia, tundra areas, northern Mongolia, Manchuria, Ussuri, Amur.
■ Natural Treasure No. 324.

Scops Owl in forest on Kyŏnghee University campus. Seoul. 1989. 6. 20.

Order Strigiformes/Family Strigidae

Scops Owl ●

Otus scops
Korean · Sochŏksae   20cm

Sexes similar. Two types : brown type and red type ; brown type has gray-brown with dark brown pattern on head, rufous with dark brown on back ; red type has rufous over whole body ; yellow eyes, long ear tufts.

STATUS : Common summer visitor.

HABITAT : Common throughout Korea ; during day sleeps in bushes, active at night.

DIET : Insects, spiders.

RANGE : Valley of Amur River, Sakhalin, Manchuria, Ussuri, northern China.

■ Natural Treasure No. 324.

Collarded Scops Owl at rest in forest on Kyŏnghee University campus. 1989. 1. 25.

Order Strigiformes/Family Strigidae

Collared Scops Owl •

Otus bakkamoena
Korean · Kŭnsochŏksae   24cm

Sexes similar. Brown head, back; edge of each feather black dappled with dark brown; pale gray under chin, under belly; the rest similar to back; red eyes; long ear tufts.

STATUS : Winter visitor, resident.

HABITAT : More in northern areas; daytime rests in dark forest areas; active from evening.

DIET : Small birds and mammalians, amphibians, reptiles, insects, spiders.

RANGE : Ussuri, southern and eastern Manchuria, Sakhalin, central China.

■ Natural Treasure No. 324.

Brown Hawk Owl on an old Zelkova tree. Kuksu, Kyŏnggi Province. 1989. 8. 20.

Order Strigiformes/Family Strigidae

Brown Hawk Owl ●

Ninox scutulata
Korean · Solbuŏngi   29cm

Sexes similar. Dark brown head, back, tail; white breast, belly with dark brown vertical stripe; brown horizontal lines on tail; yellow bill, feet, eyes; no ear tufts.

STATUS : Common summer visitor.
HABITAT : Narrow-leafed and deciduous trees, broad-leafed trees, forests near villages, city parks, gardens; active at night; will attack humans during breeding season; nests in tree holes, bird boxes.
DIET : Insects, bats, small birds.
RANGE : Temperate and tropical areas of Asia.
■ Natural Treasure No. 324.

Korean Wood Owl twenty day after hatching. Kyŏnggi Province. 1989. 8. 3.

Order Strigiformes/Family Strigidae

Korean Wood Owl

Strix aluco
Korean · Olpaemi 35cm

Sexes similar. Gray-brown with white spotted pattern on head, back; white with gray belly, breast; has brown horizontal lines on tail; yellowish green, down curving bill; pinkish beige feet.
STATUS : Rare resident.
HABITAT : Broad and narrow leafed trees on flat lands; sleeps in trees during day; active at night; breeds in forest in Kwangnŭng, Chinjŏp-myŏn, Namyang-ju-gun every year.
DIET : Field rats, insects, small fowl.
RANGE : Southern Manchuria.
■ Natural Treasure No. 324.

White-rumped Swifts on the wing. Chŏllanam Province. 1991. 8. 6.

Order Apodiformes/Family Apodidae

White-rumped Swift ●

Apus pacificus
Korean · K'alsae　　　　　　19.5cm

Sexes similar. Black head, back, wings; white rump and under chin; dark brown horizontal stripes on belly, breast.

STATUS : Common summer visitor.
HABITAT : Flies high sometimes alone but usually in large flocks; on cliffs of high mountains, cliffs on islands or along coasts; mates in air; breeds on cliffs in flocks.
DIET : Flies, beetles, cicadas, bees, flying insects.
RANGE : Siberia, Kamchatka Peninsula, Sakhalin, Hokkaido, Manchuria, eastern China.

Black-capped Kingfisher in search of food. Yangsuri. Kyŏnggi Province. 1987. 7. 5.

Order Coraciiformes/Family Alcedinidae

Black-capped Kingfisher ●

Halcyon pileata
Korean · Ch'ŏnghobansae   28cm

Sexes similar. Black top of head and ends of wings; blue back, tail, wings; large white pattern on wings, under chin, and neck; red feet and bill; orange breast, belly.
STATUS: Comparatively common summer visitor.
HABITAT: Alone or in pairs along brooks, rivers, streams, rice fields searching for food; nests in holes it makes in river or sand banks or in holes in trees; usually uses same nest every year.
DIET: Shellfish, reptiles, amphibians, fish, insects.
RANGE: Tropical and temperate zones of eastern Asia, Manchuria, China, Thailand, India.

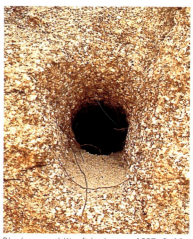

Black-capped Kingfisher's nest 1987 8 10.

Ruddy Kingfisher watching for food from branch of tree. Kyŏnggi Province. 1991. 7. 20.

Order Coraciiformes/Family Alcedinidae

Ruddy Kingfisher ●

Halcyon coromanda
Korean · Hobansae   27.5cm

Sexes similar. Whole body orange; yellowish under chin, belly; bluish gray vertical stripe on rump; thick red bill, red legs.

STATUS : Comparatively rare summer visitor.
HABITAT : Holes in trees in forests, valleys, in broad-leafed trees in mixed forests and near lakes; flies swiftly, sits quietly on tree branch beside water; kills prey by hitting it against branch of tree or rock.
DIET : Frogs, crawfish, insects.
RANGE : Japan, Manchuria; winters along coasts of Southeast Asia, Phillippines.

Ruddy Kingfisher at rest. Suipri, Yangp'yŏng-gun, Kyŏnggi Province. 1992. 6. 30.

Common Kingfisher watching for food at fish farm. Sŏngsanp'o, Cheju Island. 1989. 1. 6.

Order Coraciiformes/Family Alcedinidae

Common Kingfisher ●

Alcedo atthis
Korean · Mulch'ongsae   17cm

Sexes similar. Female lighter color than male; glossy green-blue head, shoulders, back, wings; back blue; orange behind eyes, belly, breast, feet; white throat.

STATUS : Summer visitor.
HABITAT : Throughout Korea in forests, along brooks, near reservoirs, lakes; nests in hole dug in earthen cliff; recently numbers decreasing.
DIET : Freshwater fish, amphibians, water insects.
RANGE : Baikal Lake, Amur, Ussuri, Mongolia, China, Malay Peninsula, India, Sakhalin, Japan, Taiwan.

Common Kingfisher watching for food beside lake. Kangwon Province. 1992. 10. 23.

Common Kingfisher watching for food. Sŏngsanp'o, Cheju Island. 1992. 2. 16.

Common Kingfisher watching for food on rock. Kyŏnggi Province. 1986. 8. 2.

Young Broad-billed Rollers at rest. Kuksu, Kyŏnggi Province. 1987. 8. 18.

Order Coraciiformes/Family Coraciidae

Broad-billed Roller ●

Eurystomus orientalis
Korean · Parangsae   29.5cm

Sexes similar. Red bill, feet; black wing edges, tail, head; rest dark green; large white patch on base of primaries; greenish under chin, breast, wings.

STATUS: Relatively uncommon summer visitor.

HABITAT: Forests of broad-leafed trees, mixed forests, parks in cities, near tilled fields; uses old nests of Shrikes, Woodpeckers or rotted out holes in tall, old narrow-leafed and deciduous trees.

DIET: Mainly insects.

RANGE: Japan, Amur, Ussuri, Manchuria, China, Himalayan Mountains.

Broad-billed Roller hatchlings. 1987. 8. 18.

Broad-billed Roller eggs. 1987. 8. 18.

Hoopoe holding cricket in beak. Konjiam, Kwangju-gun, Kyŏnggi Province. 1989. 8. 23.

Order Coraciiformes/Family Upupidae

Hoopoe ●

Upupa epops
Korean · Hututi   28cm

Sexes similar. Brownish yellow head, breast, upper back; black edged crest often held flat; black and white stripes on wings, tail; white belly.
STATUS: Fairly common summer visitor.
HABITAT: Rural areas, tilled fields in northern part of central areas, hills; lives in holes in tall, old trees in hills, under eaves of houses; alone or in pairs; looks for food among fallen leaves; pecks at rotten parts of trees.
DIET: Insects, larva, spiders, worms.
RANGE: Eastern Siberia, Baikal Lake, Ussuri, Manchuria.

Hoopoe two day after hatching.

◄ Broad-billed Roller in process of building nest in tall old tree. 1989. 8. 11.

Hoopoe entering nest hole in roof carrying food. Kyŏnggi Province. 1985. 6. 18.

Gray-headed Woodpecker in search of food on trunk of oak tree. Kwangnŭng. 1987. 2. 20.

Order Piciformes/Family Picidae

Gray-headed Woodpecker

Picus canus
Korean · Ch'ŏngtaktaguri   29.5cm

Male: red forehead; gray head; wings green; with black and white primaries, black mustachial stripe; white under chin, on nape; yellowish brown tail. Female: light grayish green over whole body.
STATUS: Common resident
HABITAT: Breeds in inland forests throughout country except on islands; lays eggs in holes of tall, old trees.
DIET: Insects, beetles, cicada, butterflies, locusts.
RANGE: A subspecies only in Korea.

Male Black Woodpecker protecting nest. Pŭphŭng Temple, Kangwon Province. 1990. 7. 3.

Order Piciformes/Family Picidae

Black Woodpecker

Dryocopus martius
Korean · Kamaktaktaguri   45.5cm

Male: top of head red. Female: red on back of head; whole body glossy black; greenish yellow bill with black edges.
STATUS : Rare resident.
HABITAT : From mixed tall old forest in lowlands to higher altitudes; male and female make hole in tree trunk which takes 8 to 17 days.
DIET : Insects, seeds.
RANGE : North temperate zones of Europe and Asia.
■ Natural Treasure No. 242.

Black Woodpecker guarding nest. Pŭphŭng Temple, Kangwon Province. 1988. 6. 6.

Male Black Woodpecker taking female's place on nest. Kangwon Province. 1988. 6. 6.

Black Woodpecker in search of food in old pine tree. Kangwon Province. 1992. 6. 18.

Male White-bellied Black Woodpecker in nest in tall old tree. Kyŏnggi Province. 1987. 5. 20.

Order Piciformes/Family Picidae

White-bellied Black Woodpecker

Dryocopus javensis
Korean · Kŭnaksae   46cm

Male : top of head and cheeks red ; white belly, rest glossy black ; greenish yellow bill with black tip. Female : top of head, cheeks black.

STATUS : Very rare resident.
HABITAT : Mixed forest of tall, old fir, oak and chestnut trees ; nests in tall trees, in hole it makes itself.
DIET : Beetle larva.
RANGE : Only in Korea.
- Natural Treasure No. 197.

Food for White-bellied Black Woodpecker.

White bellied Black Woodpecker searching for food. Kyŏnggi Province. 1987. 5. 2.

Female Great Spotted Woodpecker in search of food. Kyŏnggi Province. 1989. 2. 13.

Order Piciformes/Family Picidae

Great Spotted Woodpecker

Dendrocopos major
Korean · Osaektaktaguri   23.5cm

Black line from top of head to bill to upper breast ; black head, back, tail ; black and white 'V' pattern on back ; white under chin, belly ; lower belly red ; back of male's head red.
STATUS : Common resident ; commonest Woodpecker.
HABITAT : Forest alone or male and female together ; after breeding make family groups ; fly to forests or dry fields or villages ; make holes in tree trunks.
DIET : Insects, spiders, seeds.
RANGE : South central Japan.

◄ Female Great Spotted Woodpecker on guard Kwangnŭng, Kyŏnggi Province. 1992. 2. 23.

Female White-backed Woodpecker: Kwangnŭng, Kyŏnggi Province. 1987. 11. 26.

Order Piciformes/Family Picidae

White-backed Woodpecker

Dendrocopos leucotos
Korean · Kŭnosaektaktaguri 28cm

Male : top of head red. Female : top of head black. Black back and tail with white horizontal stripes on back ; white under chin, breast, belly ; lower belly pinkish.
STATUS : Rare resident.
HABITAT : Deciduous and narrow-leafed tree forests, tall old trees ; alone or in pairs.
DIET : Beetles, butterflies, bees, flies, seeds.
RANGE : From southern Arctic to temperate and sub-tropical zones.

Female White-backed Woodpecker eating magnolia seeds. Kyŏnggi Province. 1988. 11. 2. ▶

Female Dagelet White-backed Woodpecker guarding nest. Ullŭng Island. 1990. 4. 23.

Order Piciformes/Family Picidae

Dagelet White-backed Woodpecker

Dendrocopos leucotos takahashii
Korean · Uldokŭnosaektaktaguri
26cm

Sexes similar. Black bill, head back and tail; white horizontal stripes on back; white breast with vertical black pattern. Male: red from above eyes to top of head; red from breast to belly; darker on belly than on breast.
STATUS : Resident.
HABITAT : Only on Ullŭng Island; seen in villages or in nearby old trees in dry fields.
DIET : Insects, seeds.
RANGE : Sub-species of White-backed Woodpecker; lives only on Ullŭng Island.

Male Dagelet White-backed Woodpecker.

Female Dagelet White-backed Woodpecker. Sadong, Ullŭng Island. 1990. 4. 23.

Gray-headed Pygmy Woodpecker. Kwangnŭng, Kyŏnggi Province. 1991. 12. 25.

Order Piciformes/Family picidae

Gray-headed Pygmy Woodpecker

Dendrocopos canicapillus
Korean · Amulsoetaktaguri   16cm

Brownish head, cheeks; grayish white stripes on belly, breast; black with white line on back; white spot in middle of back, so easy to distinguish.

STATUS : Rare resident.
HABITAT : One seen at Forestry Experimental Station at Kwangnŭng, Kyŏnggi Province, another on an old tree on Kyŏngbok Palace grounds; during breeding season goes north or to forests in high regions.
DIET : Beetles, all kinds of insects, larvae.
RANGE : Southeastern Manchuria, valley of Ussuri.

Gray-headed Pygmy Woodpecker in search of food. Kyŏnggi Province. 1991. 12. 25.

Young Japanese Pygmy Woodpecker. Kyŏngsangnam Province. 1992. 8. 2.

Order Piciformes/Family Picidae

Japanese Pygmy Woodpecker

Dendrocopos kizuki
Korean · Soetaktaguri   15cm

Black head, back, tail; eye stripe, back of neck, back, under chin, breast, belly white; dark gray stripes on sides; back of male's head has red spots.
STATUS : Common resident throughout country.
HABITAT : In forest trees; in pairs during breeding season; in autumn and winter mix with Great Tits.
DIET : Mainly insects, seeds.
RANGE : Sakhalin, southern Kuril Archipelago, Hokkaido, Ussuri, Manchuria.

Mother and baby Japanese Pygmy Woodpecker. Kyŏngsangnam Province. 1992. 8. 1. ▶

Fairy Pitta in evergreen forest. Kŏje Island, Kyŏngsangnam Province. 1983. 8. 30.

Order Passeriformes/Family Pittidae

Fairy Pitta ●

Pitta brachyura
Korean · Palsaekcho   18cm

Sexes similar. Top of head and lower belly red; yellowish supercilium, breast and sides; green back and tail; blue shoulders and wings; black wing tips; broad black eye stripe; white spots at base of primaries.
STATUS : Rare summer visitor.
HABITAT : Alone in evergreen forests along coast; shy and rarely seen; breeds in broad-leafed trees, thickets in forests, on hillsides inland, coastal, islands.
DIET : Worms.
RANGE : Eastern China, Japan, Taiwan.
■ Natural Treasure No. 204.

Mother Skylark guarding nest. Tŭkso, Kyŏnggi Province. 1986. 6. 12.

Order Passeriformes/Family Alaudidae

Skylark

Alauda arvensis
Korean · Chongdari   17cm

Sexes similar. Top of head, breast, cheeks, back, tail brown with dark brown stripes; pale brown eye stripe, under chin, belly; edges of tail white; pinkish brown bill and legs.
STATUS : Common resident.
HABITAT : Reclaimed land, hills, tilled fields; in spring, autumn male and female together; in winter move in flocks of 30 or 40; builds nest on ground in grassy fields on riversides, in barley fields, wheat fields; when returning to nest shakes body back and forth; flight erratic; soars.
DIET : Grass seeds, grain, beetles, bees, butterflies, larvae.
RANGE : Europe, northwestern Africa, Eurasia, Ussuri, eastern Siberia, Japan.

Skylark eggs. Tŭkso. 1986. 5. 2.

Bank Swallow. Kyŏnggi Province. 1983. 8. 22.

Order Passeriformes/Family Hirundinidae

Bank Swallow •

Riparia riparia
Korean · Kalsaekchebi   12.5cm

Sexes similar. Head, back of neck, back, tail, feet brown; white under chin, breast and belly; short forked tail.
STATUS : Rare transient.
HABITAT : Sometimes seen with House Swallows going south in autumn on Kanghwa Island, Kyŏnggi Province; rests on pear farms, in reed beds.
DIET : Beetles, cicadas, flies.
RANGE : Southeastern Siberia, valley of Amur, Sakhalin, Kuril Archipelago, Hokkaido.

Male House Swallow looking for female. Kyŏngsangnam Province. 1986. 5. 8.

Order Passeriformes/Family Hirundinidae

House Swallow ●

Hirundo rustica
Korean · Chebi   17cm

Sexes similar. Forehead, under chin brown; white breast, belly, under tail; glossy green-black head, back, tail; white pattern on tip of tail.

House Swallow eggs. Kimp'o. 1992. 8. 3.

STATUS : Common summer visitor.

HABITAT : Throughout Korea; fields near villages, build nests on houses or other buildings; returns to and repairs same nest every year.

DIET : Flies, beetles.

RANGE : Central basin of Amur, valley of Ussuri, Manchuria, Mongolia, China, northern Myanmar, eastern Himalayas, Japan.

Flock of House Swallows at rest. Kanghwa-gun, Kyŏnggi Province. 1988. 8. 1.

Mother and baby House Swallows in nest under eaves. Kyŏnggi Province. 1991. 8. 17.

House Swallows eating insects from straw roof. Kanghwa-gun, Kyŏnggi Province. 1988. 8. 1.

Red-rumped Swallows resting on power line. Kyŏnggi Province. 1991. 8. 13.

Order Passeriformes/Family Hirundinidae

Red-rumped Swallow ●

Hirundo daurica
Korean · Kwijebi   18.5cm

Sexes similar. Top of head, back, wings, tail black; rufous cheeks, rump and lower belly; yellowish brown under chin, breast; belly has black vertical streaks.
STATUS : Common summer visitor.
HABITAT : Central areas; builds bottle shaped clay and straw nests under eaves of houses and temples, under bridges and roofs of buildings.
DIET : Beetles, cicadas, flies.
RANGE : Manchuria, valley of Ussuri, China, Japan.

Red-rumped Swallow eggs. 1991. 8. 30.

Forest Wagtail on tree. Kyŏngsangnam Province. 1992. 8. 2.

Order Passeriformes/Family Motacillidae

Forest Wagtail ●

Dendronanthus indicus
Korean · Mullesae   15.5cm

Sexes similar. Gray brown head, cheeks, back; white eye stripe; two white lines on black wings; white neck, breast, belly; 'T' shaped black pattern on breast.

STATUS : Common summer visitor.

HABITAT : Common in villages or in broad-leafed trees near villages; sits on tree tops, tree branches or on rocks calling and bobbing tail.

DIET : Mainly beetles, locusts

RANGE : Southern Sakhalin, Ussuri, Manchuria, northern Japan.

◀ Red-rumped Swallow. Hwado-myŏn, Namyangju-gun, Kyŏnggi Province. 1991. 8. 13.

Yellow Wagtail. Chinjuk, Poryŏng-gun, Ch'ungch'ŏngnam Province. 1987. 10. 5.

Order Passeriformes/Family Motacillidae

Yellow Wagtail ●

Motacilla flava
Korean • Kinbaltophalmisae
16.5cm

Sexes similar. Cheeks, back, top of head dark gray; black wings, tail; yellow eye stripe, under chin; belly becomes light cream color in winter; blackish gray pattern under chin on young birds.
STATUS : Rare transient.
HABITAT : Large flocks when on the move; moves tail up and down incessantly; flies in gentle up and down pattern.
DIET : Insects, spiders, molluscs.
RANGE : Southeastern Siberia, coast of Okhotsk Sea, lower Amur, Sakhalin.

Yellow Wagtails at rest. Chinjuk, Ch'ungch'ŏngnam Province. 1987. 10. 5.

Female Yellow Wagtail at rest on coast during northern migration. 1992. 4. 14.

Male Gray Wagtail in search of food in rice field. Kyŏnggi Province. 1987. 5. 7.

Order Passeriformes/Family Motacillidae

Gray Wagtail •

Motacilla cinerea
Korean • Noranghalmisae   20cm

Dark gray head, back; black wing edges, tail; yellow breast, belly; white supercilium and chin stripe. Male: black under chin. Female: white under chin.
STATUS : Common summer visitor.
HABITAT : Inland streams in valleys; builds nest on ground or in low tree.
DIET : Fly larvae, beetles, butterflies, locusts, spiders.
RANGE : Kamchatka Peninsula, coast of Okhotsk Sea, Kuril Archipelago, Sakhalin, eastern Amur area, Ussuri.

Gray Wagtail eggs. 1987. 7. 3.

Female Gray Wagtail with prey in bill. Yangp'yŏng-gun, Kyŏnggi Province. 1988. 7. 12.

White-faced Wagtail at rest on rock. Yangp'yŏng-gun, Kyŏnggi Province. 1987. 7. 12.

Order Passeriformes/Family Motacillidae

White-faced Wagtail •

Motacilla alba leucopsis
Korean • Allakhalmisae   21.5cm

Sexes similar. Back of head, breast, back, tail black; white cheeks, belly, wings; black bill, legs; also some black on wings.
STATUS : Common summer visitor.
HABITAT : Stream and riversides, tilled fields, hillsides; builds nest on hills near streams on ground; bowl shaped nest.
DIET : Spiders, insects.
RANGE : Eastern Amur area, Manchuria, western Ussuri, southern Mongolia, China, Taiwan, Japan.

White-faced Wagtail. Kanghwa-gun, Kyŏnggi Province. 1987. 7. 8.

White-faced Wagtail stretching wing. Kanghwa-gun, Kyŏnggi Province. 1987. 7. 8.

White-faced Wagtail preening. Yesan-gun, Ch'ungch'ŏngnam Province. 1986. 5. 20.

White-faced Wagtail flapping wings. Yangp'yŏng-gun, Kyŏnggi Province. 1989. 5. 23.

White Wagtail at rest on a rock on coast. Kosŏng-gun, Kangwon Province. 1980. 1. 21.

Order Passeriformes/Family Motacillidae

White Wagtail •

Motacilla alba lugens
Korean · Paekhalmisae   21cm

Sexes similar. Back of head, back, tail, beside eyes, breast black; white forehead, cheeks, wings, belly; back becomes dark gray and black on breast becomes less in winter.

STATUS : Rare winter visitor.

HABITAT : Rocks on coasts, tilled fields, sandy areas; male and female always together; seen in small groups of 2 or 3 in winter; sits on rocks, trees, electric wires or roofs of houses, when calling.

DIET : Mainly insects, spiders.

RANGE : Kamchatka Peninsula, Kuril Archipelago, Sakhalin, Amur, Ussuri, northern Japan.

Pied Wagtail in search of food along the coast. Kangwon Province. 1990. 1. 21.

Order Passeriformes/Family Motacillidae

Pied Wagtail ●

Motacilla alba ocularis
Korean · Kŏmŭntŏkhalmisae 21cm

Sexes similar. Bill, eye stripe, back of head, under chin, breast, wing edges, tail, feet black; dark gray back; white cheeks, forehead, sides, belly.
STATUS : Rare transient seen in small numbers every year under Yang Bridge, Ch'ŏngch'o Lake, Sokch'o, Kangwon Province.
HABITAT : Coasts, estuaries, beside wide streams, in flat areas, around reservoirs.
DIET : Spiders, insects.
RANGE : From northeastern Siberia to the coast of Arctic Ocean.

Japanese Wagtail calling beside stream. Ulchin, Kyŏngsangbuk Province. 1991. 7. 3.

Order Passeriformes / Family Motacillidae

Japanese Wagtail

Motacilla grandis
Korean・Kŏmŭndŭnghalmisae
21cm

Sexes similar. Back of head, cheeks, back, wing edges, tail, bill, feet black; eye stripe, under chin, belly, wings white; whole body of young birds dark gray.
STATUS : Rare resident.
HABITAT : Namyangju-gun, Kyŏnggi Province, and upper Han River, Misari; male and female together all through year.
DIET : Insects, spiders.
RANGE : Japan.

Japanese Wagtail in search of food. 1991. 7. 3.

Indian Tree Pipit at rest in a tree during migration. Kyŏnggi Province. 1981. 5. 28.

Order Passeriformes/Family Motacillidae

Indian Tree Pipit •

Anthus hodgsoni
Korean · Hingdungsae　　15.5cm

Sexes similar. Greenish gray with black pattern on top of head, cheeks, back, tail ; yellowish white eye stripe, under chin, belly ; black stripes on belly to breast.
STATUS : Common transient.
HABITAT : Common from central to southern area ; more in autumn than in spring ; high areas of Paektu Mountain ; mainly in rice fields, dry fields, sesame fields.
DIET : Insects, spiders, grass seeds.
RANGE ; Siberia, Mongolia, Kamchatka Peninsula, Kuril Archipelago, Japan, China, Himalayas.

◄ Male Japanese Wagtail. Ulchin, Kyŏngsangbuk Province. 1990. 8. 6.

Water Pipit in barley field in winter. Taebori, Kyŏngsangbuk Province. 1990. 2. 18.

Order Passeriformes/Family Motacillidae

Water Pipit •

Anthus spinoletta
Korean • Patchongdari   16cm

Sexes similar. Winter : Pale brown head, back, tail ; white under chin, belly ; yellow-brown breast, sides with dark brown pattern ; in summer belly becomes pinkish ; back blackish gray.
STATUS : Common transient, can be considered winter visitor.
HABITAT : Especially common near Yang Bridge Ch'ŏngch'o Lake, Sokch'o, Kangwon Province, Ŭlsuk Island, Pusan, in dry fields on Kŏje Island, rice fields, dry fields, beside streams sandy areas.
DIET : Insects, spiders, seeds.
RANGE : Southern Kamchatka, Kuril Archipelago, Sakhalin, southeastern Siberia.

Water Pipit in search of food. Chunam Reservoir, Kyŏngsangnam Province. 1992. 1. 23. ▶

Brown-eared Bulbul commonly seen near villages. Pŏmŏ Temple, Pusan. 1989. 3. 1.

Order Passeriformes/Family Pycnonotidae

Brown-eared Bulbul

Hypsipetes amaurotis
Korean · Chikpakkuri 27.5cm

Sexes similar. Chestnut cheeks; gray head; tips of feathers white; gray breast; blackish brown spots on belly; dark brown back, tail; black bill, feet.
STATUS : Common resident; breeds in south central areas to southern Hwanghae Province.
HABITAT : Broad-leafed forests, evergreen forests, bamboo groves along south coast.
DIET : Insects, fruits.
RANGE : Taiwan, Ryukyus, Luzon in Philippines.

Brown-eared Bulbul in search of food. Pŏmŏ Temple, Pusan. 1989. 3. 1.

Brown-eared Bulbul eating fruit. Pŏmŏ Temple, Tongnae-gu, Pusan. 1989. 3. 1.

Brown-eared Bulbul eating cherries. Sadong, Ullŭng Island. 1988. 8. 6.

Thick-billed Shrike guarding nest. Sudaeul, Kyŏnggi Province. 1991. 8. 13.

Order Passeriformes/Family Laniidae

Thick-billed Shrike ●

Lanius tigrinus
Korean · Ch'iktaekach'i   18.5cm

Sexes similar. Male's head bluish gray; female's head gray; rufous back, tail with black scales; white under chin, breast, belly: dark brown stripes on female's sides; wide black eye mask.
STATUS: Common summer visitor.
HABITAT: Bushes, tall trees in city suburbs, rural areas, hills, forests; hangs prey on barbs of barbed wire fences or on thorns or sharp twigs.
DIET: Insects, snakes, frogs, spiders, eggs of small birds.

Thick-billed Shrike eggs. 1980. 7. 20.

RANGE: Ussuri, southern Manchuria, Japan, China.

Thick-billed Shrike in search of food. Munhori, Kyŏnggi Province. 1992. 8. 5.

Female Bull-headed Shrike in search of food. Kangwon Province. 1990. 7. 25.

Order Passeriformes/Family Laniidae

Bull-headed Shrike

Lanius bucephalus
Korean · Taekach'i   20cm

Male : reddish brown head; dark gray back; black wings and tail; white spot on wings; black mask below thin white supercilium; white breast, belly. Female: whole body rufous and brown with scale pattern on belly.
STATUS : Resident ; breeds throughout country.
HABITAT : Shrubby forests in winter.
DIET : Insects, spiders, snakes, shellfish, amphibians, fish, bats, rodents, small birds.

Baby Bull-headed Shrike. 1990. 8. 15.

RANGE : Southern Ussuri, southern Manchuria, Sakhalin, Japan.

Brown Shrike in search of food. Yesan-gun, Ch'ungch'ŏngnam Province. 1991. 8. 8.

Order Passeriformes/Family Laniidae

Brown Shrike ●

Lanius cristatus
Korean • Norangtaekach'i 20cm

Sexes similar. Top of head and back gray-brown; wing edges black, in female mixed with brown; black eye mask; white supercilium, stripe under chin, breast, belly; yellowish sides; female has scale shaped pattern on sides.
STATUS : Common summer visitor.
HABITAT : Rural areas, city suburbs, hills, tilled fields, small forests; calls or watches for prey from tops of tall trees.
DIET : Insects, bats, spiders, amphibians, small birds.
RANGE : Southern Manchuria, eastern China, Kyushu in Japan.

◀ Bull-headed Shrike in winter. Chinyang Lake, Kyŏngsangnam Province. 1987. 1. 30.

Northern Shrike in search of food. Tongsong, Kangwon Province. 1989. 2. 28.

Order Passeriformes/Family Laniidae

Northern Shrike •

Lanius excubitor
Korean • Kŭnjaegaegumari
24.5cm

Sexes similar. Top of head and back gray; black eye mask; black wings, tail; wing edges white; white supercilium; white under chin, breast, belly, cheeks.
STATUS: Rare winter visitor in Kyŏnggi or Kangwon Provinces; alone or in pairs.
HABITAT: Forests; sits straight on tall trees or on tops of shrubs.
DIET: Rodents, frogs, lizards, insects, spiders, small birds.
RANGE: Sakhalin, Kuril Archipelago.

Flock of Bohemian Waxwings in winter. Kanghwa-gun, Kyŏnggi Province. 1989. 2. 17. ▶

Bohemian Waxwing eating tree seeds. Kanghwa-gun, Kyŏnggi Province. 1989. 2. 17.

Order Passeriformes/Family Bombycillidae

Bohemian Waxwing •

Bombycilla garrulus
Korean • Hwangyŏsae   19.5cm

Sexes similar. Whole body brownish; red cheeks; eye line, under chin, wings black; gray belly; tail bluish gray with yellow.
STATUS : Common winter visitor.
HABITAT : City parks, school grounds, in flocks of 20 to 40 to several hundred in hills along coast on Kanghwa Island; lives in narrow-leafed or broad-leafed tree forests.
DIET : Seeds, especially rose hips; Chinese Juniper; insects.
RANGE : Taiga in Siberia.

Bohemian Waxwings at rest in tree. Kanghwa-gun, Kyŏnggi Province. 1989. 2. 17.

Japanese Waxwing as rarely seen with flock of Bohemian Waxwings. 1989. 2. 17.

Order Passeriformes/Family Bombycillidae

Japanese Waxwing ●

Bombycilla japonica
Korean • Hongyŏsae   17.5cm

Sexes similar. Whole body brown; red cheeks; yellowish belly; black eye line, under chin; bluish black on wings; tip of tail red.

STATUS : Rare winter visitor.
HABITAT : School grounds, parks with persimmon trees, Chinese Juniper, Kwangnŭng, Kyŏnggi Province, golf course in Anyang; dozens of flocks in forests of narrow-leafed or broad-leafed trees.
DIET : Seeds and leaves.
RANGE : Downstream of Amur River, northern Ussuri, southeastern Siberia.

Japanese Waxwings in winter. Kwangju-gun, Kyŏnggi Province. 1987. 3. 2.

Winter Wren in search of food in an old tree. Pŏmŏ Temple, Pusan. 1989. 3. 2.

Order Passeriformes/Family Troglodytidae

Winter Wren

Troglodytes troglodytes
Korean • Kultuksae   10.5cm

Sexes similar. Whole body dark brown; many black spots on back, wings, tail; some white on belly; throat, legs reddish brown; many gray-brown spots on cheeks; short, cocked tail.

STATUS : Common resident.
HABITAT : Alone or male and female together in shrubby forests, on rocks in streams, on cliffs looking for food; flies around and under house eaves; calls from rocks or tops of trees; breeds under eaves of houses, in cracks of buildings, cliffs, tops of tall trees, cracks in rocks.
DIET : Beetle larvae, imago, eggs of flies, spiders.
RANGE : Amur, Sakhalin, Ussuri, Manchuria.

Winter Wren wintering near house in village. Miruji, Kyŏnggi Province. 1990. 3. 12.

Winter Wren catching insects from under a rock in a stream. Kyŏnggi Province. 1992. 2. 12.

Female Siberian Bluechat at rest near coast. Chŏllanam Province. 1986. 4. 27.

Order Passeriformes/Family Muscicapidae (Subfamily Turdinae)

Siberian Bluechat ●

Tarsiger cyanurus
Korean • Yuritaksae   14cm

Male : blue head, shoulders, back ; white under chin, breast, belly ; rufous sides. Female : white eye ring ; rufous sides ; blue tail ; brown head, breast and back.

STATUS : Migrating transient throughout country ; winters in Korea.

HABITAT : Forests near rice fields, inland areas, seen on Pukhan Mountain, Kyŏngbok Palace during cold winter.

DIET : Insects, spiders, seeds.

RANGE : Southern Siberia, Amur, Ussuri, Manchuria, Mongolia, Sakhalin, Kamchatka, Japan.

Young male Siberian Bluechat in early spring. Kyŏnggi Province. 1988. 3. 21. ▶

First Gray Bushchat observed in Korea. Taech'ŏng Island, Kyŏnggi Province. 1987. 5. 5.

Order Passeriformes/Family Muscicapidae (Subfamily Turdinae)

Gray Bushchat ○

Saxicola ferrea
Korean · Kŏmŭnpyamtaksae
14.5cm

Male : top of head light gray ; black cheeks, back, wings, bill, feet ; cream colored breast, belly.
Female : all light brown.
STATUS : Not yet officially recorded ; seen first on 5 May 1987 on Taech'ŏng Island, Ongjin-gun, Kyŏnggi Province.
HABITAT : Tilled fields along coast, weedy areas.
DIET : Insects.
RANGE : Central and northeastern Asia, desert regions, plains.

Male Daurian Redstart guarding nest. Yangp'yŏng-gun, Kyŏnggi Province. 1992. 8. 4.

Order Passeriformes/Family Muscicapidae (Subfamily Turdinae)

Daurian Redstart

Phoenicurus auroreus
Korean · Taksae 14cm

Male: top of head silvery; black cheeks, chin, wings with white spots on wings; red breast, belly, tail and rump. Female: whole body brown; lower belly, tail and rump reddish.

STATUS : Common resident; breeds throughout country.
HABITAT : Near houses, temples in high places up to 1000m; has wide range.
DIET : Beetles, butterflies, bees, flies, cicadas, seeds.
RANGE : Amur, southeastern Siberia, Mongolia, Manchuria, Ussuri, northern China.

Female Daurian Redstart guarding nest. P'och'ŏn-gun, Kyonggi Province. 1984. 5. 28.

Male Daurian Redstart eating tree seeds. Pŏphŭng Temple, Kangwon Province. 1988. 1. 29.

Female Daurian Redstart resting in tree. P'och'ŏn-gun, Kyŏnggi Province. 1984. 5. 28.

Stonechat in winter. Mi Lake, Ch'ŏngwon-gun, Ch'ungch'ŏngnam Province. 1989. 8. 5.

Order Passeriformes/Family Muscicapidae (Subfamily Turdinae)

Stonechat •

Saxicola torquata
Korean · Kŏmŭntaksae   13cm

Male: black head, back, wings, tail; red breast; sides of neck, back, wing edges, belly, rump white. Female: sides of neck, breast, waist red; rest brown with black stripes.
STATUS: Common summer visitor.
HABITAT: Rice fields, dry fields near forests, thickets on hills and on flat land, cemeteries, orchards; builds nest in grassy areas where there is shrubbery; in separate pairs even during summer.

Stonechat eggs. Mi Lake. 1989. 7. 5.

DIET: Insects.
RANGE: East central Siberia, northern Mongolia, southern Amur, Ussuri, northern China.

Female Stonechat resting on tree. Kwangju-gun, Kyŏnggi Province. 1986. 7. 5.

Male Stonechat guarding nest. Yesan-gun, Ch'ungch'ŏngnam Province. 1985. 5. 21.

Male Blue Rockthrush at rest. Mallip'o, Ch'ungch'ŏngnam Province. 1983. 7. 15.

Order Passeriformes/Family Muscicapidae(Subfamily Turdinae)

Blue Rockthrush

Monticola Solitarius
Korean • Padajikpakkuri   22.5cm

Male : glossy blue head breast, back, tail ; black wings ; rufous belly. Female : dark gray spotted head, back ; brown belly with dark brown scale pattern.
STATUS : Common resident.
HABITAT : reefs along coast, rocks, cliffs ; male and female separate each occupying own territory ; builds nest in cracks in rocky walls, in reefs, holes in cliffs, openings in buildings.
DIET : Insects, lizards, shellfish, beetles.

Female Blue Rockthrush. 1987. 4. 26.

RANGE : Southern Ussuri, Manchuria, northern China, Japan.

Mother White's Ground Thrush feeding baby birds. Chŏngnŭng, Seoul. 1988. 7. 8.

Order Passeriformes/Family Muscicapidae (Subfamily Turdinae)

White's Ground Thrush ●

Turdus dauma
Korean · Horangjipagwi   29.5cm

Sexes similar. Yellowish brown head, back, wings, with dark brown and black scale pattern; white under chin, breast, belly; black and yellow-brown scale patterns on breast, sides.
STATUS : Common summer visitor.
HABITAT : Searches for food on ground; easily distinguished from distance because of unique call; very noisy when flying.
DIET : Insects, spiders, molluscs, Annelid, worms, tree seeds.
RANGE : Southern Siberia, Manchuria, valley of Ussuri, Japan.

Brooding Mother White's Ground Thrush.

Gray-backed Thrush in thick forest. P'ogok-myŏn, Yongin-gun, Kyŏnggi Province. 1985. 7. 18.

Order Passeriformes/Family Muscicapidae (Subfamily Turdinae)

Gray-backed Thrush •

Turdus hortulorum
Korean · Toejipagwi   23cm

Male: dark gray head, breast, back, tail; white belly; red sides.
Female: white breast with dark gray spot and stripe patterns on sides; yellow-brown bill, legs.
STATUS: Common transient; summer visitor.
HABITAT: Breeds in small groups in forests; very shy; calls from early morning to late evening; beautiful voice.
DIET: Insects, seeds.
RANGE: Southeastern Siberia, Amur, northeastern Manchuria, Ussuri.

Pale Thrush eating seeds of shrub. Sŏngsan, Cheju Island. 1992. 4. 26.

Order Passeriformes/Family Muscicapidae (Subfamily Turdinae)

Pale Thrush •

Turdus pallidus
Korean • Hinbaejipagwi　　　24cm

Male : dark gray head ; brown back, tail ; black wing tips ; brownish gray-white belly. Female : chestnut head ; under chin, breast, belly white with brown spots ; tip of tail white ; yellow-brown bill and feet.
STATUS : Common summer visitor.
HABITAT : Male and female together in summer ; migrate in large flocks ; more strongly defensive than Gray-backed Thrush ;

Pale Thrush eggs. 1987. 7. 10.

builds nest on twigs of not very tall trees ; winters on islands of south coast.
DIET : Seeds, insects, spiders.
RANGE : Amur basin, Ussuri, Tsushima in Japan.

Dusky Thrush in search of food. Pugok-myŏn, Kyŏngsangnam Province. 1987. 2. 13.

Order Passeriformes/Family Muscicapidae(Subfamily Turdinae)

Dusky Thrush ●

Turdus naumanni eunomus
Korean · Kaetongjipagwi　　24cm

Sexes similar. Two color types; white eye stripe, white or cream colored chin; dark brown head, back; rufous wings; white breast, belly; one type has large black pattern on breast, the other almost no pattern.
STATUS : Common winter visitor; winters throughout country.
HABITAT : Riversides, hills, forests, bushes near rice fields, dry fields; winters in smaller groups than Naumann's Thrush.
DIET : Insects, seeds, fruits.
RANGE : Kamchatka Peninsula, northern Siberia, Sakhalin.

Dusky Thrush at rest in tree. Tongmakri, Kanghwa-gun, Kyŏnggi Province. 1990. 1. 15.

Dusky Thrush eating seeds. Tongmakri, Kanghwa-gun, Kyŏnggi Province. 1990. 1. 16.

Naumann's Thrush in search of food. Chŏndŭng Temple, Kyŏnggi Province. 1990. 1. 16.

Order Passeriformes/Family Muscicapidae(subfamily Turdinae)

Naumann's Thrush ●

Turdus naumanni naumanni
Korean · Norangjipagwi   21cm

Sexes similar. Crown, cheeks, back, tail dark brown; rufous eye stripe, breast, sides, both sides of tail; much grayish white, rufous brown spots on breast, sides; gray-white under chin, belly.
STATUS : Common winter visitor.
HABITAT : Tilled fields, city, suburbs, hills, mountainous land; searches for food on ground, in trees; greater number than Dusky Thrush, migrates in groups of 20.
DIET : Insects, seeds, fruit.
RANGE : Kamchatka Peninsula, northern Siberia, Sakhalin.

Naumann's Thrush in tree in winter. Yongin-gun, Kyŏnggi Province. 1985. 7. 18. ▶

Vinous-throated Parrotbill guarding nest. Ch'ungch'ŏngbuk Province. 1979. 4. 26.

Order Passeriformes/Family Muscicapidae (Subfamily Paradoxornithnae)

Vinous-throated Parrotbill

Paradoxornis webbiana
Korean · Pulgŭnmŏriomoknuni
13cm

Sexes similar. Dark brown head, wings, bill; rest grayish brown; relatively long tail.
STATUS: Common resident; breeds throughout Korea.
HABITAT: Grassy land, bushes, shrubs, reedy fields; forms flocks of 30 or more in winter; thick forests of Chinese Juniper, in gardens, grassy places, farm house walls.

Vinous-throated Parrotbill eggs. 1979. 6. 10.

DIET: Insects, spiders, seeds.
RANGE: China.

Flock of Vinous-throated Parrotbills. Tongduch'ŏn, Kyŏnggi Province. 1986. 2. 14.

Vinous-throated Parrotbill in search of grass seeds. Kyŏngsangnam Province. 1987. 2. 3.

Male Bush Warbler on guard. Chŏkmok, Kap'yŏng-gun, Kyŏnggi Province. 1990. 5. 29.

Order Passeriformes/Family Muscicapidae (Subfamily Sylviinae)

Bush Warbler ●

Cettia diphone
Korean · Hwiparamsae   15.5cm

Sexes similar. Grayish brown all over body; cream colored eye stripe; base of bill and feet yellow-brown.

STATUS : Common summer visitor; breeds throughout country.
HABITAT : Streamsides near rice fields, dry fields, bushes on hillsides, low trees near villages; builds nests in shrubby areas, grasslands, bamboo groves; alone or in pairs, does not form flocks.
DIET : Insects.
RANGE : Southern Ussuri, southeastern Manchuria.

◄ Vinous-throated Parrotbill at rest in bush. Kyŏngsangnam Province. 1987. 2. 3.

Island Grasshopper Warbler guarding nest. Kyŏngsangnam Province. 1991. 8. 21.

Order Passeriformes/Family Muscicapidae (Subfamily Sylviinae)

Island Grasshopper Warbler ●

Locustella ochotensis pleski
Korean · Sŏmgaegaebi   16cm

Sexes similar. Dark brown back, rump, tail, sides, head, wings; white neck, breast, belly.
STATUS : Common summer visitor.
HABITAT : Breeds on islands of west and southeast coasts; hides in reeds, thickets; searches for food on ground, on rocks; seen on Ullŭng Island in Kyŏngsangbuk Province, on Kŏje Island in Kyŏngsangnam Province, on Sasu Island, Island, Pukchŏju-gun, Cheju Hoenggan Island.
DIET : Insects, seeds.
RANGE : Japan.

◄ Male Bush Warbler in search of food. Munhori, Kyŏnggi Province. 1992. 6. 14.

Female Great Reed Warbler at nest. Yangp'yŏng-gun, Kyŏnggi Province. 1987. 8. 1.

Order Passeriformes/Family Muscicapidae (Subfamily Sylviinae)

Great Reed Warbler ●

Acrocephalus arundinaceus
Korean · Kaegaebi   18.5cm

Sexes similar. Brown head, back, wings, tail; dark brown wing tips; grayish white under chin, breast, belly; light brown sides; yellow-brown bill; green-gray legs.

STATUS : Summer visitor.
HABITAT : Breeds in reed beds throughout the country except in island areas and high mountains; in reed beds, along rivers, around reservoirs; builds nest in reeds, on branches of broad-leafed tree.
DIET : Insects, amphibians, molluscs.
RANGE : Eastern Mongolia, valley of Amur, valley of Ussuri, Japan, China.

Great Reed Warbler in riverside reed bed. P'aju, Kyŏnggi Province. 1987. 8. 13.

Arctic Warbler resting during migration. Soch'ŏng, Kyŏnggi Province. 1988. 8. 23.

Order Passeriformes/Family Muscicapidae (Subfamily Sylviinae)

Arctic Warbler ●

Phylloscopus borealis
Korean · Soesolsae   13cm

Sexes similar. Green-gray top of head, cheeks; brownish wings and tail; yellowish white supercilium, breast, belly; three or four white spots on shoulders.
STATUS : Migratory transient; throughout country.
HABITAT : Trees; never goes to ground for food; suburbs of Seoul, P'och'ŏn, Kwangnŭng in Kyŏnggi Province, Kanghwa Island.
DIET : Insects, seeds.
RANGE : Northern area of Japan, eastern China during migration.

Crowned Willow Warbler singing. Yanggu-gun, Kangwon Province. 1989. 8. 16.

Order Passeriformes/Family Muscicapidae (Subfamily Sylviinae)

Crowned Willow Warbler ●

Phylloscopus occipitalis
Korean · Sansolsae   12.5cm

Sexes similar. Green-gray head, cheeks, back, tail; creamy greenish supercilium; white under chin, breast, belly; thin black crown stripes; short pale cream wing bar on closed wing; yellow-brown feet.

STATUS : Rare summer visitor; breeds throughout country.

HABITAT : Breeds in broadleafed trees, builds nest on ground, in cliffs.

DIET : Insects.

RANGE : Valley of Amur, valley of Ussuri, Manchuria, Japan.

Order Passeriformes/Family Muscicapidae (Subfamily Muscicapinae)

Tricolor Flycatcher ●

Ficedula zanthopygia
Korean · Hinnunsŏphwanggŭmsae
13cm

Male: black head, back, tail; white eyebrow, white patch on wing; yellow under chin, breast, belly. Female: gray-brown head, back, tail; brown scale pattern on grayish white breast.
STATUS : Common summer visitor.
HABITAT : Throughout country in small forests, city parks, gardens, on flat lands, hills, in broad-leafed trees and in mixed forests; will use manmade nests.
DIET : Imago, insect larvae.
RANGE : Eastern Siberia, valley of Amur, Ussuri, Manchuria, eastern China.

Male Tricolor Flycatcher in thick forest. Kyŏngg

Male Tricolor Flycatcher with food for young. Kyŏnggi Province. 1992. 7. 9.

Province. 1991. 7. 2.

Female Tricolor Flycatcher at rest. Yangp'yŏng-gun, Kyŏnggi Province. 1992. 7. 9.

Male Blue and White Flycatcher calling female. Kangwon Province. 1990. 6. 13.

Order Passeriformes/Family Muscicapidae (Subfamily Muscicapinae)

Blue and White Flycatcher ●

Cyanoptila cyanomelana
Korean · Kŭnyurisae   16.5cm

Male : top of head, back, wings, tail blue ; cheeks, under chin, breast, black ; white belly.
Female : dark brown head, breast, back, tail ; white under chin, belly.
STATUS : Common summer visitor.
HABITAT : In thickly forested valleys in tall trees, near rice fields and dry fields ; male and female remain together and form family group after breeding period.
DIET : Insects, spiders.
RANGE : Japan.

Long-tailed Tit guarding nest. Campus of Seoul Agricultural University. 1983. 7. 18.

Order Passeriformes/Family Aegithalidae

Long-tailed Tit

Aegithalos caudatus
Korean • Omoknuni   13.5cm

Sexes similar. Top of head, under chin, breast, belly white; black cheeks, back, wings, tail; pinkish shoulders and lower belly; black bill, legs.
STATUS : Common resident throughout country.
HABITAT : Male and female together during breeding season and then form family group, build nests in fallen leaves in broadleafed tree forests, in pine trees and shrubs.
DIET : Insects, spiders, seeds.

Long-tailed Tit's nest. 1984. 6. 6.

RANGE : Siberia, Okhotsk Sea coast, Amur, Sakhalin, Iran, northern Mongolia, Ussuri, Japan, China.

Marsh Tit as commonly seen in forest. Kwangnŭng, Kyŏnggi Province. 1990. 1. 2.

Order Passeriformes/Family Paridae

Marsh Tit

Parus palustris
Korean · Soebaksae   12.5cm

Sexes similar. Top of head, under chin black; gray back, wings, tail; grayish white cheeks, breast, belly.
STATUS : Common resident breeding in all areas except on remote islands.
HABITAT : Lives in thick forests or alpine regions in breeding season. In winter goes down to flat land and areas around houses in cities. Breeds in natural holes in tree trunks or old woodpecker nests.
DIET : Insects, spiders, seeds.
RANGE : Northern China, Manchuria.

Coal Tit in forest during winter. Kwangnŭng, Kyŏnggi Province. 1990. 1. 2.

Order Passeriformes/Family Paridae

Coal Tit

Parus ater
Korean · Chinbaksae   11cm

Sexes similar. Head, chin, neck, tail black; white cheeks, nape, breast, belly; dark gray back; two white stripes on wings; brown sides to breast.
STATUS : Common resident everywhere except on islands.
HABITAT : Thick forests in smaller groups than Marsh Tits; prefers high hills, high mountainous areas.
DIET : Insects, spiders, seeds.
RANGE : Northern Amur, Sakhalin, Mongolia, China, Japan, Himalayas, Taiwan.

Varied Tit as commonly seen in thick forests. Kwangnŭng, Kyŏnggi Province. 1987. 4. 2.

Order Passeriformes/Family Paridae

Varied Tit

Parus Varius
Korean · Konjulbagi 14cm

Sexes similar. Forehead, cheeks, nape, cream colored; top of head, side of neck, chin black; red breast, belly; back, wings, tail bluish gray.
STATUS : Common resident.
HABITAT : Thick forests, thickets; lays eggs in natural holes in tree trunks, in cracks of buildings; inhabited regions; will use manmade nests.
DIET : Insects, spiders, seeds.
RANGE : Japan, southern Kuril Archipelago.

Varied Tit in search of food. Puphŭng Temple, Kangwon Province. 1983. 5. 13. ▶

Great Tit, most commonly seen in forests. Kwangnŭng, Kyŏnggi Province. 1990. 1. 3.

Order Passeriformes/Family Paridae

Great Tit

Parus major
Korean · Paksae   14.5cm

Sexes similar. White cheeks, nape, belly; top of head, around cheeks, line from under chin down belly, wing tips, tail black; green-gray back with yellowish upper part; black stripe on belly with male's broader than female's.
STATUS : Common resident.
HABITAT : Breeds throughout country including Cheju Island, Ullŭng Island; male and female remain together during breeding season; in winter mix with Coal Tits, Marsh Tits, Nuthatchs in forests.
DIET : Insects, spiders, seeds.
RANGE : Valley of Amur, valley of Ussuri, Manchuria, Japan.

Great Tit eating seeds. Kwangnŭng, Namyangju-gun, Kyŏnggi Province. 1990. 1. 3.

Great Tit in search of food. Kwangnŭng, Namyangju-gun, Kyŏnggi Province. 1990. 1. 3.

Nuthatch which usually lives on old trees. Kyŏnggi Province. 1990. 1. 3.

Order Passeriformes/Family Sittidae

Nuthatch

Sitta europaea
Korean · Tongobi   13.5cm

Sexes similar. Top of head, wings, tail bluish gray; white cheeks, under chin, breast, belly; rufous sides; eye stripe, wing tips black.
STATUS : Common resident
HABITAT : Breeds in thick forests; almost never seen on ground; lives on tree trunks characteristically upside down.
DIET : Insects, spiders, seeds and fruits.
RANGE : Southern valley of Amur, Manchuria, Japan, valley of Ussuri.

Nuthatch in search of insects. Kwangnŭng, Kyŏnggi Province. 1990. 1. 26.

Nuthatch eating beef tallow and lard in winter. Kyŏnggi Province. 1990. 2. 1.

Japanese White-eye eating camellia nectar in early spring. Pusan. 1990. 3. 14.

Order Passeriformes/Family Zosteropidae

Japanese White-eye

Zosterops japonica
Korean・Tongbaksae   11.5cm

Sexes similar. Head, back, wings, tail yellowish green; brown breast, sides; white belly; yellow chin, under tail; white ring around eye.
STATUS : Resident.
HABITAT : Breeds along southern and east coasts in evergreen forests; forms flocks after breeding season.
DIET : Spiders, ticks, insects, beetles, camellia and plum blossoms, nectar, seeds including those of magnolia.
RANGE : Japan.

Japanese White-eye eating strawberry. Pŏmŏ Temple. 1990. 3. 14.

Japanese White-eye eating bread. Pŏmŏ Temple, Pusan. 1990. 3. 14.

Japanese White-eye eating outer covering of ripe fruit of Machilus thunbergii. Hŭksan Island,

Chŏllanam Province. 1991. 7. 28.

Female Siberian Meadow Bunting in early spring. Chŏllanam Province. 1987. 5. 5.

Order Passeriformes/Family Emberizidae

Siberian Meadow Bunting

Emberiza cioides
Korean · Metsae   16.5cm

Male's cheeks black, female's dark brown; crown, back, tail, breast, rufous; supercilium, chin, cheek patch, belly white.
STATUS : Common resident.

HABITAT : Grassy fields, bushes near rice fields, dry fields, on hills rather than in mountains; male and female together except during winter and migration; strongly territorial during breeding season; shrubby forests, grassy ground, thickets, pine tree forests.
DIET : Weed seeds, larva, imago.
RANGE : Southern Siberia, valley of Amur, Mongolia, Manchuria, valley of Ussuri, Japan, China.

Male Siberian Meadow Bunting in winter. Kyŏngsangnam Province. 1988. 2. 11.

Female Japanese Reed Bunting in winter. Tongsong, Kangwon Province. 1990. 12. 2.

Order Passeriformes/Family Emberizidae

Japanese Reed Bunting •

Emberiza yessoensis
Korean · Soegŏmŭnmŏrisuksae
14.5cm

Male has black head in summer, female's is rufous; in winter eye stripe, breast, belly light brown; back, wings, tail rufous; black stripes and spots under chin.
STATUS : Common winter visitor.
HABITAT : Thickets on flat land, reclaimed land, small forests, reed beds; in winter on rice fields in marshes in groups looking for food.
DIET : Insects, seeds.
RANGE : Eastern Mongolia, Manchuria, Ussuri, northern China.

Tristram's Bunting at rest during northward migration. Kyŏnggi Province. 1985. 5. 10.

Order Passeriformes/Family Emberizidae

Tristram's Bunting ●

Emberiza tristrami
Korean · Hinbaemetsae   15cm

Male has black head, female's is dark brown; white supercilium, crown shaped chin stripe, cheek patch, belly; back brown with black stripes; rufous breast, tail, rump.
STATUS : Common transient.
HABITAT : Tall trees, bushy forests, thickets near tilled land, reclaimed land; mixes with Chestnut Bunting, Siberian Black-faced Bunting; finds food on ground in forest, on trees.
DIET : Insects, seeds.
RANGE : Central valley of Amur, valley of Ussuri, Manchuria.

Gray-headed Bunting claiming territory. Kimp'o-gun, Kyŏnggi Province. 1973. 7. 21.

Order Passeriformes/Family Emberizidae

Gray-headed Bunting •

Emberiza fucata
Korean • Pulgŭnpyammetsae
16cm

Sexes similar. Top of head dark gray; pale brown with black and brown stripes on back; cheeks, shoulders, rump and tail red; white chin; black horizontal stripes on breast.
STATUS : Common summer visitor throughout country.
HABITAT : Banks of rivers; low bushes on hills, scrub near rice fields, dry fields, public cemeteries.
DIET : Spiders, insects, seeds.
RANGE : Northern Mongolia, central Amur, Manchuria, valley of Ussuri, China, Japan.

◄ Tristram's Bunting, rarely seen as here in central area. Kyŏnggi Province. 1985. 5. 10.

Little Bunting in winter near rice field. Kyŏngsangnam Province. 1987. 2. 8.

Order Passeriformes/Family Emberizidae

Little Bunting ●

Emberiza pusilla
Korean · Soebulgŭnpyammetsae
12.5cm

Sexes similar. Summer: rufous head, shoulders, wings; black crown, stripes around cheeks; gray-brown back, dark brown stripes all over body; in winter rufous on head disappears.
STATUS : Comparatively rare transient.
HABITAT : Moves in large and small flocks; sometimes mixes with Rustic Buntings; low shrubs and bushes; searches for food on ground.
DIET : Insects, seeds.
RANGE : Eastern Siberia.

◄ Gray-headed Bunting guarding nest. Mi Lake, Ch'ungch'ŏngbuk Province. 1992. 6. 1.

Rustic Bunting in winter. Kanghwa-gun, Kyŏnggi Province. 1992. 2. 13.

Order Passeriformes/Family Emberizidae

Rustic Bunting ●

Emberiza rustica
Korean · Suksae   15cm

Summer(male) : black head. Winter : brown head ; supercilium, chin, belly white ; back brown with black stripes ; reddish brown breast, sides, rump.
STATUS : Common winter visitor.
HABITAT : Around tilled areas, hills, forests in flocks of 20 to 30 or 100 to 200 birds.
DIET : Weed seeds, larva, imago.
RANGE : Kamchatka Peninsula ; winters in Korea, Japan, eastern China.

Rustic Bunting at rest. Kwangnŭng, Namyangju-gun, Kyŏnggi Province. 1983. 3. 11.

Rustic Bunting eating seeds. Sudaeul, Yangp'yŏng-gun Kyŏnggi Province. 1983. 2. 9.

Male Yellow-throated Bunting in winter in thicket. Kyŏnggi Province. 1990. 3. 2.

Order Passeriformes/Family Emberizidae

Yellow-throated Bunting

Emberiza elegans
Korean · Norangtŏkmetsae 15.5cm

Male: black around eyes, cheeks, breast, short crest; yellow chin. Female: brown around eyes, cheeks; light brown breast, chin; top of head, short crest dark brown; yellow supercilium and nape; white belly; rest brown with rufous and black pattern.
STATUS: Common resident.
HABITAT: Hills, rice fields, dry fields; builds nest on twigs in forest or on ground.
DIET: Seeds, larva, imago.
RANGE: Middle and down stream on Amur River, Ussuri, Manchuria, Japan.

Male Yellow-throated Bunting claiming territory. Kangwon Province. 1987. 8. 30.

Male Chestnut Bunting. P'ogok-myŏn, Yongin-gun, Kyŏnggi Province. 1986. 6. 3.

Order Passeriformes/Family Emberizidae

Chestnut Bunting •

Emberiza rutila
Korean • Kokachamsae   13.5cm

Male : rufous head, breast, back, rump ; yellow belly ; gray brown with black stripes on wings and tail. Female : pale brown with dark brown streaks on crown, back, cheeks, tail ; yellow with dark brown streaks on cheeks, chin, breast, belly.
STATUS : Common transient.
HABITAT : Millet, sesame fields ; in flocks of 20 to 30 or several hundred ; searches for food on ground.
DIET : Weed seeds, cereals, insects.
RANGE : Coast of Okhotsk Sea, downstream on Amur River, southern Siberia.

Female Chestnut Bunting resting in millet field. Kyŏnggi Province. 1988. 10. 20.

Male Chestnut Bunting eating millet. Kyŏnggi Province. 1988. 10. 20.

Siberian Black-faced Bunting at rest. Kanghwa-gun, Kyŏnggi Province. 1989. 6. 21.

Order Passeriformes/Family Emberizidae

Siberian Black-faced Bunting •

Emberiza spodocephala
Korean • Ch'oksae   16cm

Sexes similar. Gray from forehead to back of neck ; brown back with black stripes ; gray chin ; light yellowish brown with brown streaks on breast, belly, sides.
STATUS : Common transient.
HABITAT : Shrubby forests, thickets near fields, forests of narrow-leafed trees ; from lowlands to high mountains, reclaimed land ; lakes, rivers, streams, brookside areas, swamps.
DIET : Weed seeds, cereals, insects.
RANGE : Southern Siberia, Amur, Ussuri, Manchuria.

Reed Bunting in winter. Ch'ŏrwon, Kangwon Province. 1989. 2. 13.

Order passeriformes/Family Emberizidae

Reed Bunting •

Emberiza schoeniclus
Korean · Kŏmŭnmŏrisuksae 16cm

Sexes similar. Summer : head, chin black ; rufous back, wings with black stripes ; chin stripe collar, belly white. Winter : rufous with black pattern on head, back, wings ; brown chin, breast has black stripes.

STATUS : Rare winter visitor.

HABITAT : Fields, riverside thickets, shrubby forests, weedy ground ; forms small flocks in winter.

DIET : Seeds, insects.

RANGE : Kamchatka, Kuril Archipelago, Amur, Ussuri, Hokkaido.

Brambling at rest in winter. Kyŏngsangnam Province. 1990. 1. 18.

Order Passeriformes/Family Fringillidae

Brambling •

Fringilla montifringilla
Korean · Toesae   16cm

Male's head, back, wings black ; in winter gray ; orange breast, shoulders ; white belly, rump ; female's cheeks brownish gray ; yellow bill.
STATUS : Common winter visitor.

Female Brambling. 1990. 1. 18.

HABITAT : Fields, hills, small forests, reclaimed land in groups of 10 to tens of thousands in autumn and winter ; rest in trees ; look for food on ground.
DIET : Rice, barley, corn, pine seeds, seeds of other plants, insects.
RANGE : Siberia, Okhotsk Sea, Kamchatka Penninsula, downstream on Amur River.

Flock of Bramblings. P'ap'yŏng-myŏn, P'aju-gun, Kyŏnggi Province. 1989. 2. 7.

Flock of Bramblings in winter. P'ap'yŏng-myŏn, P'aju-gun, Kyŏnggi Province. 1989. 2. 7.

Female Oriental Greenfinch. Ch'ŏnsu Bay, Ch'ungch'ŏngnam Province. 1989. 3. 3.

Order Passeriformes/Family Fringillidae

Oriental Greenfinch

Carduelis sinica
Korean · Pangulsae   14.5cm

Dark gray-brown head; brown back, breast, belly; black wings; outer tailfeathers and base of flight feathers yellow; pinkish bill, legs.
STATUS : Common resident.
HABITAT : Hills, rural areas; hills near villages; form small flocks of 20 to 30 birds in autumn and winter; search for food in fields, forests, trees near inhabited areas; larch, narrow-leafed tree forests.
DIET : Weed seeds, cereals, insects.
RANGE : Eastern Manchuria, valley of Ussuri.

Oriental Greenfinch eating unripe Indian millet. Kangwon Province. 1992. 3. 8.

Male Oriental Greenfinch eating grass seeds. Sadong, Ullŭng Island. 1990. 4. 22.

Siskin in winter. Taehŭng-myŏn, Ch'ungCh'ŏngnam Province. 1989. 4. 5.

Order Passeriformes/Family Fringillidae

Siskin ●

Carduelis spinus
Korean · Kŏmŭnmŏribangulsae
12.5cm

Male : forehead, crown, chin black ; breast, upper belly yellow. Female : white chin, breast, upper belly ; yellow sides ; green back with black stripes : black wings with two yellow stripes.
STATUS : Common winter visitor.
HABITAT : Cities, suburbs, rural areas, hills ; in narrow-leafed forests ; flock size changes every year, more than ten to several hundred ; live in trees.
DIET : Tree seeds including pine tree seeds, seeds of other plants.
RANGE : Siberia, Europe, Ussuri, Sakhalin, Japan.

◄ Flock of Oriental Greenfinchs. Ch'ŏnsu Bay, Ch'ungch'ŏngnam Province. 1989. 3. 3.

Scarlet Finch hiding in grass during migration. Chŏllanam Province. 1992. 8. 20.

Order Passeriformes/Family Fringillidae

Scarlet Finch ○

Carpodacus erythrinus
Korean · Chŏkwonja   14cm

Male : red head, breast, rump. Female : gray-brown head, rump ; whitish breast ; white belly ; gray-brown back, tail ; male's tail darker than female's.
STATUS : Rare stray ; passes through in spring and autumn in small groups.
HABITAT : Shrubs, thickets on reclaimed land, fields, hills, foot of mountains ; seen occasionally in weedy areas along coast of Sohŭksan Island, Shinan-gun, Chŏllanam Province.
DIET : Weed and tree seeds, sprouts of shrubs, insects.
RANGE : Kamchatka Peninsula, eastern Siberia, Okhotsk Sea, northern Mongolia, Amur, Ussuri, Sakhalin, Manchuria.

Male Pallas' Rosy Finch in winter Kwangnŭng, Kyŏnggi Province. 1983. 3. 18.

Order Passeriformes/Family Fringillidae
Pallas' Rosy Finch ●

Carpodacus roseus
Korean・Yangjini   17.5cm

Male : head, back, breast, belly red ; white spots on forehead, chin, cheeks. Female : brown over whole body ; black wings, tail ; white lower belly, under tail.
STATUS : Common winter visitor.
HABITAT : Small forests, hills around fields, in compounds, bushes everywhere in small or large groups.
DIET : Millet, rice plants, bean seeds, fruit of tea plants, plantain seeds, insects.
RANGE : Northern Baikal Lake, Sakhalin.

Pallas' Rosy Finch eating grass seeds. Kyŏnggi Province. 1988. 2. 20.

Pallas' Rosy Finch on way south. P'och'ŏn-gun, Kyŏnggi Province. 1991. 2. 2.

Long-tailed Rose Finch eating seeds during winter. Kyŏnggi Province. 1989. 1. 30.

Order Passeriformes/Family Fringillidae

Long-tailed Rose Finch •

Uragus sibiricus
Korean • Kinkorihongyangjini
15cm

Male ; crown brown ; two stripes on wings ; eyes, chin, breast, belly red but in winter become light. Female ; brown over whole body.
STATUS : Occasional visitor in south central areas in winter.
HABITAT : Seen beside streams, foot of mountains, tilled land, hills, reclaimed land, shrubby thickets, low forests, grass.
DIET : Small insects, seeds and fruit.
RANGE : Valley of Ussuri, central Manchuria.

Bullfinch eating seeds. Kwangnŭng, Namyangju-gun, Kyŏnggi Province. 1974. 1. 2.

Order Passeriformes/Family Fringillidae

Bullfinch •

Pyrrhula pyrrhula
Korean · Mŭtchangisae 15.5cm

Male : crown, wings, tail black ; white stripe on wing ; red cheeks, chin ; rest gray ; rump white. Female : cheeks, chin, breast, belly brown ; gray pattern on wings.

STATUS : Rare winter visitor.
HABITAT : In small groups in winter and spring ; lives in trees and goes to ground for water or to bathe ; in forests near rice fields and inland forests near streams.
DIET : Young sprouts, leaves, seeds, insects.
RANGE : Downstream of Amur, valley of Ussuri, Sakhalin.

Male Chinese Grosbeak. P'ogok-myŏn, Yongin-gun, Kyŏnggi Province. 1981. 8. 5.

Order Passeriformes/Family Fringillidae

Chinese Grosbeak ●

Eophona migratoria
Korean · Milhwaburi   18.5cm

Male: from chin to crown, wings, tail black; bluish on wings and tips of primaries; grayish brown body; orange sides to belly; pale rump. Female: Gray-brown head, tail; yellow bill.
STATUS: Common summer visitor.
HABITAT: Small stands of trees in cities, suburbs, in compound forests; male and female together during breeding season, other times in flocks in broad-leafed tree forests.
DIET: Seeds, cereals, insects.
RANGE: Southern valley of Amur, valley of Ussuri, Manchuria.

Chinese Grosbeak eggs. Tŭkso. 1986. 7. 21.

Male and female Chinese Grosbeaks bathing. Kyŏnggi Province. 1980. 7. 8.

Chinese Grosbeak seemingly lost during migration. Kyŏngbok Palace, Seoul. 1980. 12. 1.

Chinese Grosbeak eating Indian millet during migration. Kyŏnggi Province. 1989. 10. 3.

Female Hawfinch in winter. P'ogok-myŏn, Yongin-gun, Kyŏnggi Province. 1983. 1. 17.

Order Passeriformes/Family Fringillidae

Hawfinch ●

Coccothraustes coccothraustes
Korean · Kongsae   18cm

Top of head, cheeks rufous ; black in front of eye, chin, wings, tail ; white stripe on wing ; chestnut back ; side of neck gray ; breast, belly brown.

STATUS : Comparatively common winter visitor.
HABITAT : Thick forests near fields, in forests on hills, in seed beds and windbreak forests near fields ; in small flocks or alone.
DIET : Fruit, tree seeds, insects.
RANGE : Europe, southwestern Siberia, northern Mongolia, valley of Amur, Manchuria, Ussuri, southern Kuril Archipelago.

Male Russet Sparrow in search of food. Ullŭng Island. 1990. 8. 14.

Order Passeriformes/Family Ploceidae

Russet Sparrow

Passer rutilans
Korean · Sŏmch'amsae   14cm

Female Russet Sparrow. 1990. 8. 13.

Male : crown back rufous with black stripes ; black wings and tail ; grayish white cheeks, breast, belly. Female : brown head, back ; eye stripe, chin, belly cream colored.
STATUS : Common resident.
HABITAT : Forests, fields, hills, east coast and south coast islands, in winter drift about in inland areas ; during breeding season male and female together or with family ; forms flocks in winter and autumn ; nests in holes of tall trees in villages.
DIET : Rice, millet, insects.
RANGE : Southern Sakhalin, China, northern Japan.

Male Russet Sparrow carrying food. Ullŭng Island. 1990. 8. 14.

Russet Sparrow unique to Ullŭng Island. Chŏdong, Ullŭng Island. 1990. 8. 13.

Tree Sparrow at rest on tree branch. Bigŭm Island, Chŏllanam Province. 1989. 4. 26.

Order Passeriformes/Family Ploceidae

Tree Sparrow

Passer montanus
Korean · Ch'amsae   14.5cm

Sexes similar. Head, back, wings chestnut; black stripes on back, in front of eye, chin, spot on cheeks; cheeks, side of neck white; gray-brown belly, breast; female lighter color than male.
STATUS : Common resident.
HABITAT : Throughout country except Ullŭng Island, on remote islands, in cities, suburbs, fields, hills, low mountains; nests in bird houses, under tiles, in cracks of buildings, in holes in power line poles.
DIET : Insects, cereals, grass seeds, tree fruits.
RANGE : Manchuria, Ussuri, valley of Amur.

Daurian Myna guarding nearby nest. Campus of Seoul Agricultural College. 1980. 8. 7.

Order Passeriformes/Family Sturnidae

Daurian Myna ●

Sturnus sturninus
Korean · Pukbangsoechirŭregi
16.5cm

Male: gray head, breast, belly; black spot on back of head; pink rump; black back, wings, tail; glossy green, yellow-brown stripes on wings. Female: gray-brown head, breast, belly; black-brown back, wings.
STATUS: Rare summer visitor; breeds in north central areas of country.
HABITAT: Golf course in Anyang, Kyŏnggi Province, on campus of Seoul Agricultural College; builds nests in bird houses, in cracks of buildings, in power line poles.
DIET: Tree fruits, insects.
RANGE: China, Manchuria, Ussuri, Amur.

◂ Tree Sparrow in field after breeding season. Ch'ungch'ŏngnam Province. 1987. 2. 5.

①~② : Female Daurian Myna feeding nestlings in hole on power line pole. 1988. 8. 7.

Female Daurian Myna at rest. Campus of Seoul Agricultural College. 1988. 8. 1.

Courting pair of Gray Starlings. Kwangnŭng, Kyŏnggi Province. 1988. 6. 20.

Order Passeriformes/Family Sturnidae

Gray Starling ●

Sturnus cineraceus
Korean・Chirŭregi   24cm

Sexes similar. Black head, breast, back, tail; white cheeks, tip of tail, rump, belly; gray-brown sides; base of bill, feet orange; bill tip black.

STATUS : Common summer visitor.
HABITAT : City parks, gardens, school grounds, fields, hills, temples; after breeding goes south in flocks in winter to Kyŏngsangnam, Chŏllanam Provinces, Cheju Island in small numbers.
DIET : Amphibians, molluscs, rats, insects, wheat, barley, peas, cherries.
RANGE : Valley of Amur, Ussuri, Manchuria.

Gray Starling in search of food. Kangwon Province. 1989. 7. 26.

Gray Starling with green frog in its mouth. Kyŏnggi Province. 1988. 8. 13.

Gray Starling in search of food. Puk-myŏn, Kap'yŏng-gun, Kyŏnggi Province. 1990. 6. 20.

Female Black-naped Oriole feeding nestlings. Ch'ungch'ŏngnam Province. 1990. 7. 10.

Order Passeriformes/Family Oriolidae

Black-naped Oriole ●

Oriolus chinensis
Korean · Koekori　　　　　26cm

Sexes similar. Red bill; line from front of eye to back of head, wing tips, tail black; rest bright yellow; the male brighter than the female.

STATUS: Common summer visitor throughout country except Ullŭng Island.
HABITAT: Broad-leafed trees in hills rather than on high mountains, forests, parks, around temples; alone or male and female together.
DIET: Cherries, wild berries, wild grapes, insects.
RANGE: Amur, Manchuria, Ussuri, China.

Male Black-naped Oriole in search of food in forest. Kyŏnggi Province. 1990. 8. 30. ▶

Young Black-naped Oriole. Namyangju-gun, Kyonggi Province. 1990. 8. 30.

Eggs of Black-naped Oriole. Yesan-gun, Ch'ungch'ongnam Province. 1990. 7. 1.

Jay at rest on a tree. Kwangnŭng, Namyangju-gun, Kyŏnggi Province. 1988. 4. 5.

Order Passeriformes/Family Corvidae

Jay

Garrulus glandarius
Korean · Ŏch'i 33cm

Sexes similar. Brown head; black stripes on crown; cheek stripe, wings black; white and blue pattern on wings; gray-brown back; pinkish brown breast and belly; blue wing coverts.
STATUS : Common resident.
HABITAT : Throughout country except remote islands; in thick forests and on high mountains rather than on hills and in fields; same as oak tree in its range.
DIET : Eggs, baby birds, amphibians, lizards, fish, rice plants, corn, acorns.
RANGE : Southern Siberia, northern Mongolia, Sakhalin, Hokkaido.

Jay in search of food. Kwangnŭng, Namyangju-gun, Kyŏnggi Province. 1988. 4. 5.

Jay in search of acorns. Kwangnŭng, Namyangju-gun, Kyŏnggi Province. 1988. 4. 5.

Azure-winged Magpie eating tree seeds. Kyŏnggi Province. 1989. 3. 14.

Order Passeriformes/Family Corvidae

Azure-winged Magpie

Cyanopica cyana
Korean · Mulkach'i   37cm

Sexes similar. Bill, crown wing tips, feet black; blue wings; tail white; dark gray back, belly; light gray cheeks, chin.
STATUS: Common resident; breeds in inland areas.
HABITAT: From hills to high mountains; in flocks usually of 5 to 10 birds except during breeding season.
DIET: insects, amphibians, fish, rice plants, beans, corn, potatos, pears, persimmons, oranges.
RANGE: Eastern China, Manchuria, northern Japan.

Black-billed Magpie on guard at top of a tree. Kyŏngsangnam Province. 1989. 2. 18.

Order Passeriformes/Family Corvidae

Black-billed Magpie

Pica pica
Korean · Kach'i   45cm

Sexes similar. Bill, head, breast, back, wings, lower belly, tail black; glossy blue-green wings, tail; edge of back, wings, belly white.

STATUS : Very common resident; breeds throughout country.
HABITAT : City gardens, villages; mainly in low areas; rarely seen in remote high mountains, remote islands.
DIET : Eggs of small birds, nestlings, small fish, snakes, amphibian, insects, barley, rice, beans, apples, grapes, garbage.
RANGE : Amur, Ussuri, Manchuria, China, Taiwan.

◄ Azure-winged Magpie in thick forest during breeding season. Inje-gun. 1989. 8. 23.

White Black-billed Magpie, very rare. Ch'ungch'ŏngbuk Province. 1989. 8. 23.

White Black-billed Magpie eating a frog. Ch'ungch'ŏngbuk Province. 1989. 8. 23.

Black-billed Magpie. Yangp'yŏng-gun, Kyŏnggi Province. 1989. 1. 29.

Mother Black-billed Magpie on guard near nest. Ilsan, Kyŏnggi Province. 1987. 12. 8.

Rooks eating barley in dry field. Cheju Island. 1989. 2. 4.

Order Passeriformes/Family Corvidae

Rook •

Corvus frugilegus
Korean • Tekamagwi   47cm

Sexes similar. Whole body glossy black; dark gray bill; base of bill light gray-brown.
STATUS : Winter visitor.

HABITAT : Forests, fields near villages; in cities, in trees; seen in large flocks in fields near villages in Kyŏngsangnam Province and on Cheju Island.
DIET : Eggs and baby birds, small fish, insects, beans, potatos, fruits.
RANGE : Southern Siberia, northern Mongolia, valley of Amur, Manchuria, southern China.

Carrion Crow in search of food in rice field. Kyŏngsangbuk Province. 1983. 5. 15.

Order Passeriformes/Family Corvidae

Carrion Crow

Corvus corone
Korean · Kamagwi   50cm

Sexes similar. Whole body glossy black.
STATUS : Common resident.
HABITAT : Throughout country in narrow-leafed forests from low lands to remote mountains in flocks in winter ; appears in flocks along waterways, on riversides, and estuaries.
DIET : Eggs and baby birds, rats, farm crops, fruit, shellfish, insects, garbage.
RANGE : Siberia, Kamchatka, Kuril Archipelago, Sakhalin, Japan, China, Mongolia, Manchuria, Amur, Ussuri, northern Afghanistan, northern Iran.

Nest of Carrion Crow and eight day old babies. Ch'ungch'ŏngbuk Province. 1985. 6. 4.

Carrion Crows in search of food. Tongsong, Ch'ŏrwon-gun, Kangwon Province. 1992. 2. 8.

Carrion Crown preening. Taech'ŏng Island, Ongjin-gun, Kyŏnggi Province. 1987. 8. 23.

APPENDIX

- Korean Birds Designated Natural Treasures, Their Breeding Areas, Habitats
- Korean Birds 396 Species
- Scientific Names
- English Names
- References

Korean Natural Treasure Birds

A brief description of some of the birds which are official Natural Monuments follows.

1. Well known Korean species and their range.
2. Special groups and their range or the places from which they come.
3. Very rare birds that are in need of protection and their range.
4. Special Korean domestic animals.
5. Location of very rare animals, specimens, and fossils especially of those which are scientifically important.

Of the fifty one designated natural treasures, forty three are related to birds. Twenty of the natural treasures are bird species, such as the White-bellied Black Woodpecker; one is the breeding area of the White Silky Fowl, Gallus Domesticus, and twenty two are bird habitats.

The author did not get pictures of some of the species, among which were several of the birds designated natural treasures, so they are not included in the guide.

Korean Birds Designated Natural Treasures, Their Breeding Areas, Habitats, Ranges

(★—The author was unable to get pictures of these)

Number	Name	Location	Date of Designation
11	Kwangnŭng, habitat of White-bellied Black Woodpecker	Pup'yŏngri, Chinjŏp-myŏn, Namyangju-gun, Kyŏnggi Province	1962. 12.3.
13	Gray Heron breeding area, Chinch'ŏn	Nowonri Iwol-myŏn, Chinch'ŏn-gun, Ch'ungch'ŏngbuk Province	1962. 12.3.
★101	Swan's Winter habitat, Jin Island	Coastal area, Tŏkpyongri, Kunnae-myŏn, and Suryuri, Chindo-ŭp, Chindo-gun, Chŏllanam Province	1962. 12.3.
179	Migratory bird range, downstream on the Naktong River	Chinhae City, Changwon-gun, Chinhae-gun, Kyŏngsangnam Province and one part of Pusan City	1966. 7.13.
197	White-bellied Black Woodpecker	Throughout country	1968. 5.30.
★198	Japanese Crested Ibis	Throughout country	1968. 5.30.
199	White Stork	Throughout country	1968. 5.30.
★200	Black Stork	Throughout country	1968. 5.30.
201	Swans (Mute Swan, Whooper Swan, Whistling Swan)	Throughout country	1968. 5.30.

202	Manchurian Crane	Throughout country	1968. 5.30.
203	White-naped Crane	Throughout country	1968. 5.30.
204	Fairy Pitta	Throughout country	1968. 5.30.
205	Family Threskiornithidae(Spoonbill, Black-faced Spoonbill)	Throughout country	1968. 5.30.
*206	Great Bustard	Throughout country	1968. 5.30.
*208	Egret & Gray Heron breeding area, Hak Island, Samch'ŏnp'o	To-dong, Samch'ŏnp'o, Kyŏngsangnam Province	1968. 7.18.
209	Egret & Gray Heron breeding area in Shinjŏpri, Yŏju	Shinjŏpri, Puknae-myŏn, Yŏju-gun, Kyŏnggi Province	1968. 7.18.
*211	Egret & Gray Heron breeding area	Yongwolri, Muan-ŭp, Muan-gun, Chŏllanam Province	1968. 7.18.
215	Japanese Wood Pigeon	Throughout country	1968. 11.20.
227	Winter habitat of Gaviidae family, Kŏje Island coastal area	Throughout country	1970. 10.30.
228	Hooded Crane	Throughout country	1970. 10.30.
229	Egret & Gray Heron breeding area in Pomaeri, Yangyang	P'omaeri, Hyŏnnam-myŏn, Yangyang-gun, Kangwon Province	1970. 11.5.

231	Egret & Gray Heron breeding area in Tosŏnri, T'ongyŏng	Tosŏnri, Tosan-myŏn, T'ongyŏng-gun, Kyŏngsangnam Province	1970.11.5.
233	Camelia & Fairy Pitta breeding area in Hak-dong	Hakdongri, Tongbu-myŏn, Kŏje-gun, Kyŏngsangnam Province	1971. 9.13.
237	Japanese Wood Pigeon habitat in Sa-dong, Ullŭng Island	Sa-dong, Nam-myŏn, Ullŭng Island, Kyŏngsangbuk Province	1971. 12.14.
242	Black Woodpecker	Throughout country	1973. 4.12.
243	Family Accipitridae(Black Vulture, Golden Eagle, Steller's Sea-Eagle, White-tailed Eagle)	Throughout country	1973. 4.12.
245	Migratory bird winter habitat in Ch'ŏnt'ongri, Ch'ŏrwon	Some parts of Ch'ŏrwon-ŭp, Ch'ŏrwon-gun, Kangwon Province	1973. 7.10.
248	Egret & Gray Heron breeding area in Apkokri, Hoengsŏng	Apkokri, Sŏwon-myŏn, Hoengsŏng-gun, Kangwon Province	1973. 10.1.
250	White-naped Crane winter habitat downstream on Han River	Some part of P'aju-gun, Kyŏnggi Province	1975. 2.21.

265	White Silky Fowl in Hwaakri, Yŏnsan	Hwaakri, Yŏnsan-myŏn, Nonsan-gun, Ch'ungch'ŏngnam Province	1980. 4.1.
323	Family Falconidae (Chinese Sparrow Hawk, Sparrow Hawk, Marsh Harrier, Kestrel, Falcon) Peregrine	Throughout country	1982. 11.4.
324	Strigidae & Owls (Korean Wood Owl, Eagle Owl, Brown Hawk Owl, Long-eared Owl, Short-eared Owl, Scops Owl, Collared Scops Owl)	Throughout country	1982. 11.4.
325	Goose(Swan Goose, Brant)	Throughout country	1982. 11.4.
326	Oystercatcher	Throughout country	1982. 11.4.
327	Mandarin Duck	Throughout country	1982. 11.4.
332	Sea bird breeding area on Ch'ilbal Island(Swinhoe's Storm Petrel, Streaked Shearwater, White-rumped Swift)	The whole area of Ch'ilbal Island, Shinan-gun, Chŏllanam Province	1982. 11.4.

*333	Sea bird breeding area on Sasu Island (Japanese Wood Pigeon, Streaked Shearwater)	The whole area of Sasu Island, North Cheju-gun, Cheju Island	1982. 11.4.
334	Black-tailed Gull breeding area on Nan Island	The whole area of Nan Island, T'aean-gun, Ch'ungch'ŏngnam Province	1982. 11.4.
335	Black-tailed Gull breeding area on Hong Island	The Whole area of Hong Island, T'ongyŏng-gun, Kyŏngsangnam Province	1982. 11.4
336	Sea bird breeding area on Tok Island (Swinhoe's Storm Petrel, Black-tailed Gull)	The Whole area of Tok Island, Tori, Ullŭng-gun, Kyŏngsangbuk Province	1982. 11.4.
341	Sea bird breeding area on Kukhŭl Island (Japanese Murrelet, Swinhoe's Storm Petrel, Streaked Shearwater)	Kagŏdori, Hŭksan-myŏn, Shinan-gun, Chŏllanam Province	1984. 8.13.
360	Chinese Egret & Black-tailed Gull breeding area on Shin Island	The whole area of Shin Island, Changbongri, Pukto-myŏn, Ongjin-gun, Kyŏnggi Province	1988. 8.23.
361	Chinese Egret	Throughout country	1988. 8.23.

No. 11. Kwangnŭng, habitat of White-bellied Black Woodpecker

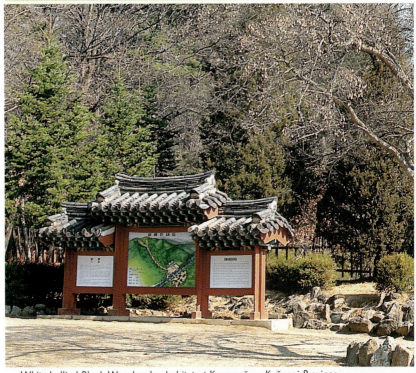

White-bellied Black Woodpecker habitat at Kwangnŭng, Kyŏnggi Province

Information signboard

White-bellied Black Woodpecker

No. 13. Gray Heron breeding area, Chinch'ŏn

Gray Heron

Information signboard

A ginkgo tree in which Gray Herons nest in Chinch'ŏn

No. 179. Migratory bird range, downstream on the Naktong River

Swans' winter habitat downstream on Naktong River, Ŭlsuk Island

Group of gulls wintering on Ŭlsuk Island

Group of Bean Geese visiting Ŭlsuk Island

No. 197. White-bellied Black Woodpecker

White-bellied Black Woodpecker searching for food in an old oak tree

No. 199. White Stork

Widow White Stork sitting on unfertilized egg

No. 201. Swans

Whistling Swans

Group of Whooper Swans in winter

Mute Swan

Group of Mute Swans wintering on Ch'ŏngch'o Lake in Sokch'o

No. 202. Manchurian Crane

A pair of Manchurian Cranes

Group of Manchurian Cranes

No. 203. White-naped Crane

White-naped Cranes in rice field in winter

No. 204. Fairy Pitta

Fairy Pitta

No. 205. Family Threskiornithidae

Group of Black-faced Spoonbills

Spoonbill

No. 209. Egret & Gray Heron breeding area in Shinjŏpri, Yŏju

Egret & Gray Heron breeding area

Information signboard

Great Egret's eggs

Many Great Egrets live in Shinjŏpri in Yŏju

No. 215. Japanese Wood Pigeon

Japanese Wood Pigeon

No. 227. Winter habitat of family Gaviidae, Kŏje Island coastal area

Red-throated Diver in winter

Gaviidae winter habitat on Kŏje Island

No. 228. Hooded Crane

Group of Hooded Cranes in winter

No. 229. Egret & Gray Heron breeding area in P'omaeri, Yangyang

Gray Heron on its nest

Intermediate Egret searching for food

Great Egret breeding area in P'omaeri, Yangyang

Egret & Gray Heron breeding area in P'omaeri, Yangyang

No. 231. Egret & Gray Heron breeding area in Tosŏnri, T'ongyŏng

Gray Heron

Information signboard

Egret & Gray Heron breeding area in Tosŏnri

No. 233. Camelia & Fairy Pitta breeding area in Hak-dong

Fairy Pitta breeding area in Hak-dong, Kŏje Island

Camelias in Hak-dong

No. 237. Japanese Wood Pigeon habitat in Sa-dong, Ullŭng Island

Japanese Wood Pigeon habitat in Sa-dong, Ullŭng Island

Japanese Wood Pigeon

Information signboard

Early information signboard

No. 242. Black Woodpecker

Black Woodpecker

No. 243. Family Accipitridae

Black Vulture

Golden Eagle

Steller's Sea-Eagle

White-tailed Eagle

No. 245. Migratory bird winter habitat in Ch'ŏnt'ongri, Ch'ŏrwon

Group of White-naped Cranes in DMZ area in winter

Information signboard

Group of White-naped Cranes winters in Ch'ŏnt'ongri

Group of Manchurian Cranes in DMZ area in winter

No. 248. Egret & Gray Heron breeding area in Apkokri, Hoengsŏng

Egret & Gray Heron breeding area in Apkokri, Hoengsŏng

Information signboard

Many Intermediate Egrets live in Apkokri

No. 250. White-naped Crane winter habitat downstream on Han River

White-naped Cranes wintering in downstream on Han River

Information signboard

No. 265. White Silky Fowl in Hwaakri, Yŏnsan

White Silky Fowl breeding area in Hwaakri, Yŏnsan

Information Signboard

White Silky Fowl's eggs

No. 323. Family Falconidae

Chinese Sparrow Hawk

Marsh Harrier

Kestrel

Peregrine Falcon

No. 324. Strigidae & Owls

Korean Wood Owl's baby

Eagle Owl

Brown Hawk Owl

Long-eared Owl

Short-eared Owl

Scops Owl

Collared Scops Owl

No. 325. Goose

Swan Goose searching for food in around reservoir

Group of Brants downstream on river in winter

No. 326. Oystercatcher

Oystercatcher at rest

No. 327. Mandarin Duck

Group of Mandarin Ducks at rest in puddle in forest

No. 332. Sea bird breeding area on Ch'ilbal Island

Sea bird breeding area on Ch'ilbal Island, Shinan-gun, Chŏllanam Province

White-rumped Swift habitat in Ch'ilbal Island

Streaked Shearwater habitat in Ch'ilbal Island

No. 334. Black-tailed Gull breeding area on Nan Island

Group of Black-tailed Gulls in Nan Island breeding area, Ch'ungch'ŏngnam Province

Black-tailed Gull habitat on Nan Island

No. 335. Black-tailed Gull breeding area on Hong Island

Black-tailed Gull breeding area on Hong Island, Ch'ungmu, Kyŏngsangnam Province

Black-tailed Gull breeding area on Hong Island

Information signboard

No. 336. Sea bird breeding area on Tok Island

Sea bird breeding area on Tok Island

Black-tailed Gull breeding area in Tok Island

No. 341. Sea bird breeding area in Kukhŭl Island

Sea bird breeding area in Kukhŭl Island, Shinan-gun, Ch'ŏllanam Province

Streaked Shearwater

Swinhoe's Storm Petrel

No. 360. Chinese Egret & Black-tailed Gull breeding area on Shin Island

Chinese Egret & Black-tailed Gull breeding area on Shin Island

Information signboard

Group of Black-tailed Gulls in breeding on Shin Island

Group of Chinese Egrets at rest on seashore

No. 361. Chinese Egret

Chinese Egret

Korean birds 396 species

> **Explanatory notes**
> English Name : Red-throated Diver
> Scientific Name : *Gavia stellata stellata* (Pontoppidan)
> Status : Winter visitor   (*-Not shown in text)

ORDER GAVIIFORMES

Family Gaviidae

1. Red-throated Diver
   Gavia stellata stellata (Pontoppidan)
   Winter visitor
2. Pacific Diver
   Gavia pacifica (Lawrence)
   Winter visitor
*3. Arctic Loon
   Gavia arctica viridigularis (Dwight)
   Winter visitor
*4. Yellow-billed Loon
   Gavia adamsii (G. R. Gray)
   Winter visitor

ORDER PODICIPEDIFORMES

Family Podicipedae

5. Little Grebe

Podiceps ruficollis poggei (Reichenow)
Winter visitor
6. Eared Grebe
Podiceps nigricollis nigricollis (C. L. Brehm)
Winter visitor
*7. Horned Grebe
Podiceps auritus auritus (Linné)
Winter visitor
8. Great Crested Grebe
Podiceps cristatus cristatus (Linné)
Winter visitor
9. Red-necked Grebe
Podiceps grisegena holböllii (Reinhardt)
Winter visitor

ORDER PROCELLARIIFORMES

Family Diomedeidae

*10. Short-tailed Albatross
Diomedea albatrus (Pallas)
Accidentals and strays

Family Procellariidae

11. Streaked Shearwater
Calonectris leucomelas (Temminck)
Summer visitor
*12. Flesh-footed Shearwater
Puffinus Carneipes (Gould)
Transient
*13. Short-tailed Shearwater
Puffinus tenuirostris (Temminck)
Transient

Family Hydrobatidae

14. Swinhoe's Storm Petrel
 Oceanodroma monorhis (Swinhoe)
 Summer visitor

ORDER PELECANIFORMES

Family Pelecanidae

*15. Spot-billed Pelican
 Pelecanus philippensis crispus (Bruch)
 Accidentals and strays

Family Sulidae

*16. Brown Booby
 Sula leucogaster plotus (Forster)
 Accidentals and strays

Family Phalacrocoracidae

*17. Great Cormorant
 Phalacrocorax carbo hanedae (Kuroda)
 Winter visitor
*18. Temminck's Cormorant
 Phalacrocorax filamentosus (Temminck & Schlegel)
 Winter visitor
*19. Pelagic Cormorant
 Phalacrocorax pelagicus pelagicus (Pallas)
 Winter visitor

Family Fregatidae

*20. Lesser Frigatebird
   Fregata ariel ariel (G. R. Gray)
   Accidentals and strays

ORDER CICONIIFORMES

Family Ardeidae

21. Bittern
    Botaurus stellaris stellaris (Linné)
    Summer visitor
22. Chinese Little Bittern
    Ixobrychus sinensis sinensis (Gmelin)
    Summer visitor
*23. Schrenck's Little Bittern
    Ixobrychus eurythmus (Swinhoe)
    Summer visitor
*24. Chinese Pond Heron
    Ardeola bacchus (Bonaparte)
    Accidentals and strays
*25. Cinnamon Bittern
    Ixobrychus cinnamomeus (Gmelin)
    Accidentals and stranger
*26. Japanese Night Heron
    Gorsakius goisagi (Temminck)
    Accidentals and strays
27. Black-crowned Night Heron
    Nycticorax nycticorax nyciticorax (Linné)
    Summer visitor
28. Green-backed Heron
    Butorides striatus amurensis (Schrenck)
    Summer visitor
29. Cattle Egret
    Bubulcus ibis coromandus (Boddaert)
    Summer visitor
30. Chinese Egret

Egretta eulophotes (Swinhoe)
Summer visitor
31. Little Egret
Egretta garzetta garzetta (Linné)
Summer visitor
32. Intermediate Egret
Egretta intermedia intermedia (Wagler)
Summer visitor
33. Great Egret
Egretta alba modesta (Gray)
Summer visitor
*34. Large Egret
Egretta alba alba (Linné)
Winter visitor
35. Eastern Reef Heron
Egretta sacra sacra (Gmelin)
Resident
36. Gray Heron
Ardea cinerea jouyi (Clark)
Summer visitor
*37. Purple Heron
Ardea purpurea manilensis (Meyen)
Winter visitor

Family Ciconiidae

38. White Stork
Ciconia ciconia boyciana (Swinhoe)
Winter visitor
*39. Black Stork
Ciconia nigra (Linné)
Winter visitor

Family Threskiornithidae

*40. Japanese Crested Ibis
Nipponia nippon (Temminck)

Winter visitor
*41. Oriental Ibis
Threskironis melanocephalus (Latham)
Accidentals and strays
42. Spoonbill
Platalea leucorodia leucorodia (Linné)
Winter visitor
43. Black-faced Spoonbill
Platalea minor (Temminck & Schlegel)
Winter visitor

ORDER ANSERIFORMES

Family Anatidae

44. Brant
Branta bernicla orientalis (Tougarinov)
Winter visitor
45. White-fronted Goose
Anser albifrons frontalis (Baird)
Winter visitor
*46. Graylag Goose
Anser anser rubrirostris (Swinhoe)
Accidentals and strays
*47. Lesser White-fronted Goose
Anser erythropus (Linné)
Accidentals and strays
*48. Snow Goose
Anser caerulescens hyperboreus (Pallas)
Accidentals and strays
49. Swan Goose
Anser cygnoides (Linné)
Winter visitor
50. Bean Goose
Anser fabalis (Latham)
Winter visitor

51. Mute Swan
    Cygnus olor (Gmelin)
    Winter visitor
52. Whooper Swan
    Cygnus cygnus (Linné)
    Winter visitor
53. Whistling Swan
    Cygnus columbianus jankowskii (Alpheraky)
    Winter visitor
54. Ruddy Shelduck
    Tadorna ferruginea (Pallas)
    Winter visitor
55. Common Shelduck
    Tadorna tadorna (Linné)
    Winter visitor
*56. Crested Shelduck
    Tadorna cristato (Kuroda)
    Extinct species
57. Mallard
    Anas platyrhynchos platyrhynchos (Linné)
    Winter visitor
58. Spot-billed Duck
    Anas poecilorhyncha zonorhycha (Swinhoe)
    Resident
59. Shoveller
    Anas clypeata (Linné)
    Winter visitor
60. Teal
    Anas crecca crecca (Linné)
    Winter visitor
*61. Green-winged Teal
    Anas crecca carolinensis (Gmelin)
    Accidentals and strays
62. Garganey
    Anas querquedula (Linné)
    Winter visitor
63. Baikal Teal

    Anas formosa (Georgi)
    Winter visitor
64. Mandarin Duck
    Aix galericulata (Linné)
    Resident
65. Falcated Teal
    Anas falcata (Georgi)
    Winter visitor
66. Gadwall
    Anas strepera strepera (Linné)
    Winter visitor
67. Pintail
    Anas acuta acuta (Linné)
    Winter visitor
68. Wigeon
    Anas penelope (Linné)
    Winter visitor
69. American Wigeon
    Anas americana (Gmelin)
    Accidentals and strays
*70. Canvasback
    Aythya valisineria (Wilson)
    Accidentals and strays
71. Pochard
    Aythya ferina (Linné)
    Winter visitor
*72. Baer's Pochard
    Aythya baeri (Radde)
    Winter visitor
73. Tufted Duck
    Aythya fuligula (Linné)
    Winter visitor
74. Greater Scaup
    Aythya marila mariloides (Vigors)
    Winter visitor
75. Black Scoter
    Melanitta nigra americana (Swainson)

Winter visitor
76. White-winged Scoter
Melanitta fusca stejnegeri (Ridgway)
Winter visitor
77. Harlequin Duck
Histrionicus histrionicus (Linné)
Winter visitor
*78. Oldsquaw
Clangula hyemalis (Linné)
Winter visitor
79. Common Goldeneye
Bucephala clangula clangula (Linné)
Winter visitor
*80. Barrow's Goldeneye
Bucephala islandica (Gmelin)
Accidentals and strays
81. Smew
Mergus albellus (Linné)
Winter visitor
82. Red-breasted Merganser
Mergus serrator (Linné)
Winter visitor
83. Common Merganser
Mergus merganser merganser (Linné)
Winter visitor
*84. Chinese Merganser
Mergus squamatus (Gould)
Winter visitor

ORDER FALCONIFORMES

Family Accipitridae

85. Osprey
Pandion haliaetus haliaetus (Linné)
Winter visitor

*86. Honey Buzzard
   Pernis ptilorhynchus orientalis (Taczanowski)
   Transient
*87. Black Kite
   Milvus migrans lineatus (J. E. Gray)
   Winter visitor
 88. White-tailed Eagle
   Haliaeetus albicilla (Linné)
   Winter visitor
 89. Steller's Sea-Eagle
   Haliaeetus pelagicus pelagicus (Pallas)
   Winter visitor
*90. Goshawk
   Accipiter gentilis schvedowi (Menzbier)
   Winter visitor
 91. Chinese Sparrow Hawk
   Accipiter soloensis (Horsfield)
   Summer visitor
*92. Japanese Lesser Sparrow Hawk
   Accipiter gularis gularis (Temminck & Schlegel)
   Transient
*93. Sparrow Hawk
   Accipiter nisus nisosimilis (Tickell)
   Resident
*94. Rough-legged Buzzard
   Buteo lagopus menzbieri (Dementiev)
   Winter visitor
*95. Upland Buzzard
   Buteo hemilasius (Temminck & Schlegel)
   Winter visitor
 96. Common Buzzard
   Buteo buteo japonicus (Temminck & Schlegel)
   Resident
 97. Gray-faced Buzzard-Eagle
   Butastur indicus (Gmelin)
   Transient
*98. Hodgson's Hawk-Eagle

Spizaetus nipalensis orientalis (Temminck & Schlegel)
Accidentals and strays
*99. Spotted Eagle
Aquila clanga (Pallas)
Winter visitor
100. Imperial Eagle
Aquila heliaca heliaca (Savigny)
Winter visitor
101. Golden Eagle
Aquila chrysaetos japonica (Severtzov)
Resident
102. Black Vulture
Aegypius monachus (Linné)
Winter visitor
103. Northern Harrier
Circus cyaneus cyaneus (Linné)
Winter visitor
104. Pied Harrier
Circus melanoleucos (Pennant)
Transient
105. Marsh Harrier
Circus aeruginosus spilonotus (Kaup)
Transient

Family Falconidae

*106. Saker Falcon
Falco cherrug milvipes (Jerdon)
Accidentals and strays
*107. Falcon
Falcon peregrinus pealei (Ridgway)
Accidentals and strays
108. Peregrine Falcon
Faclo peregrinus japonensis (Gmelin)
Resident
*109. Hobby
Falco subbuteo subbuteo (Linné)

      Transient
*110. Merlin
      Falco columbarius insignis (Clark)
      Winter visitor
*111. Amur Red-footed Falcon
      Falco vespertinus amurensis (Radde)
      Transient
112. Kestrel
      Falco tinnunculus interstinctus (Horsfield)
      Resident

ORDER GALLIFORMES

Family Tetraonidae

113. Hazel Grouse
      Tetrastes bonasia vicinitas (Riley)
      Resident

Family Phasianidae

*114. Common Quail
      Coturnix coturnix japonica (Temminck & Schlegel)
      Winter visitor
115. Ring-necked Pheasant
      Phasianus colchicus karpowi (Buturlin)
      Resident

ORDER GRUIFORMES

Family Turnicidae

*116. Burmese Button Quail
      Turnix tanki blanforddii (Blyth)
      Transient

Family Gruidae

*117. Common Crane
Grus grus lilfordi (Sharpe)
Winter visitor
118. Manchurian Crane
Grus japonensis (P.L.S. Müller)
Winter visitor
119. White-naped Crane
Grus vipio (Pallas)
Winter visitor
*120. Sandhill Crane
Grus canadensis canadensis (Linné)
Accidentals and strays
121. Hooded Crane
Grus monacha (Temminck)
Winter visitor
*122. Demoiselle Crane
Anthropoides virgo (Linné)
Accidentals and strays

Family Rallidae

*123. Water Rail
Rallus aquaticus indicus (Blyth)
Transient
124. Ruddy Crake
Porzana fusca erythrothorax (Temminck & Schlegel)
Summer visitor
*125. Ballion's Crake
Porzana pusilla pusilla (Pallas)
Transient
*126. Swinhoe's Yellow Rail
Porzana exquisita (Swinhoe)
Transient
*127. Siberian Ruddy Crake
Porzana paykullii (Ljungh)

Transient
128. White-breasted Waterhen
Amaurornis phoenicurus chinensis (Boddaert)
Accidentals and strays
129. Common Gallinule
Gallinula chloropus indica (Blyth)
Summer visitor
130. Watercock
Gallicrex cinerea cinerea (Gmelin)
Summer visitor
131. Coot
Fulica atra atra (Linné)
Transient

Family Otididae

*132. Great Bustard
Otis tarda dybowskii (Taczanowski)
Winter visitor

ORDER CHARADRIIFORMES

Family Rostratulidae

*133. Painted Snipe
Rostratula benghalensis benghalensis (Linné)
Accidentals and strays

Family Haematopdidae

134. Oystercatcher
Haematopus ostralegus osculans (Swinhoe)
Resident

Family Charadriidae

*135. Ringed Plover
Charadrius hiaticula tundrae (Lowe)
Transient
136. Little Ringed Plover
Charadrius dubius curonicus (Gmelin)
Summer visitor
137. Long-billed Ringed Plover
Charadrius placidus (J. E. and G. R. Gray)
Transient
138. Kentish Plover
Charadrius alexandrinus alexandrinus (Linné)
Transient
139. Mongolian Plover
Charadrius mongolus stegmanni (Portenko)
Transient
*140. Greater Sand Plover
Charadrius leschenaultii (Lesson)
Transient
*141. Caspian Plover
Charadrius asiaticus veredus (Gould)
Accidentals and strays
142. Lesser Golden Plover
Pluvialis dominica fulva (Gmelin)
Transient
143. Black-bellied Plover
Pluvialis squatarola (Linné)
Winter visitor
144. Lapwing
Vanellus vanellus (Linné)
Winter visitor
*145. Gray-headed Lapwing
Microsarcops cinereus (Blyth)
Accidentals and strays

Family Scolopacidae

146. Ruddy Turnstone

Arenaria interpres interpres (Linné)
Transient
147. Rufous-necked Stint
Calidris ruficollis (Pallas)
Transient
148. Long-toed Stint
Calidris minutilla subminuta (Middendorff)
Transient
*149. Temminck's Stint
Calidris temminckiii (Leisler)
Transient
*150. Pectoral Sandpiper
Calidris melanotos (Vieillot)
Accidentals and strays
151. Sharp-tailed Sandpiper
Calidris acuminata (Horsfield)
Transient
152. Dunlin
Calidris alpina sakhalina (Vieillot)
Transient
153. Curlew Sandpiper
Calidris ferruginea (Pontoppidan)
Transient
*154. Red Knot
Calidris canutus rogersi (Mathews)
Transient
155. Great Knot
Calidris tenuirostris (Horsfield)
Transient
156. Sanderling
Crocethia alba (Pallas)
Transient
*157. Spoon-billed Sandpiper
Eurynorhynchus pygmeus (Linné)
Transient
*158. Buff-breasted Sandpiper
Trygnites subruficollis (Vieillot)

Accidentals and strays
*159. Ruff
Philomachus pugnax (Linné)
Accidentals and strays
160. Broad-billed Sandpiper
Limicola falcinellus sibirica (Dresser)
Transient
161. Spotted Redshank
Tringa erythropus (Pallas)
Transient
162. Redshank
Tringa totanus eurhinus (Oberholser)
Transient
163. Marsh Sandpiper
Tringa stagnatilis (Bechstein)
Transient
164. Greenshank
Tringa nebularia (Gunnerus)
Transient
*165. Spotted Greenshank
Tringa guttifer (Nordmann)
Transient
*166. Green Sandpiper
Tringa ochropus (Linné)
Transient
167. Wood Sandpiper
Tringa glareola (Linné)
Transient
168. Gray-tailed Tattler
Tringa brevipes (Vieillot)
Transient
169. Common Sandpiper
Tringa hypoleucos (Linné)
Summer visitor
170. Terek Sandpiper
Xenus cinereus (Güldenstädt)
Transient

171. Black-tailed Godwit
    Limosa limosa melanuroides (Gould)
    Transient
172. Bar-tailed Godwit
    Limosa lapponica baueri (Naumann)
    Transient
*173. Curlew
    Numenius arquata orientalis (Brehm)
    Winter visitor
174. Australian Curlew
    Numenius madagascariensis (Linné)
    Transient
175. Whimbrel
    Numenius phaeopus variegatus (Scopoli)
    Transient
*176. Little Whimbrel
    Numenius minutus (Gould)
    Transient
*177. Woodcock
    Scolopax rusticola (Linné)
    Transient
178. Common Snipe
    Gallinago gallinago gallinago (Linné)
    Transient
*179. Pintail Snipe
    Gallinago stenura (Bonaparte)
    Transient
*180. Swinhoe's Snipe
    Gallinago megala (Swinhoe)
    Transient
*181. Solitary Snipe
    Gallinago solitaria joponica (Bonaparte)
    Transient
*182. Jack Snipe
    Lymnocryptes minimus (Brüunich)
    Accidentals and strays

Family Recurvirostridae

183. Black-winged Stilt
 Himantopus himantopus himantopus (Linné)
 Accidentals and strays
*184. Avocet
 Recurvirostra avocetta (Linné)
 Accidentals and strays

Family Phalaropodidae

185. Northern Phalarope
 Phalaropus lobatus (Linné)
 Transient

Family Glareolidae

186. Indian Pratincole
 Glareola maldivarum (J. R. Forster)
 Transient

Family Laridae

187. Black-headed Gull
 Larus ridibundus sibiricus (Buturlin)
 Winter visitor
188. Herring Gull
 Larus argentatus vegae (Palmen)
 Winter visitor
189. Slaty-backed Gull
 Larus schistisagus (Stejneger)
 Winter visitor
*190. Mew Gull
 Larus canus kamtschatschensis (Bonaparte)
 Winter visitor
191. Black-tailed Gull
 Larus crassirostris (Vieillot)

Resident
*192. Saunders's Gull
Larus saundersi (Swinhoe)
Winter visitor
*193. Sabine's Gull
Larus sabini tschuktschorum (Portenko)
Accidentals and strays
194. Black-legged Kittiwake
Larus tridactylus pollicaris (Ridgway)
Winter visitor
*195. White-winged Black Tern
Sterna leucoptera (Temminck)
Accidentals and strays
*196. Sooty Tern
Sterna fuscata nubilosa (Sparrman)
Accidentals and strays
197. Common Tern
Sterna hirundo longipennis (Nordmann)
Transient
198. Little Tern
Sterna albifrons sinensis (Gmelin)
Summer visitor

Family Alcidae

*199. Guillemot
Uria aalge inornata (Salomonsen)
Winter visitor
*200. Spectacled Guillemot
Cepphus carbo (Pallas)
Winter visitor
*201. Marbled Murrelet
Brachyramphus marmoratus perdix (Pallas)
Winter visitor
202. Ancient Murrelet
Synthliboramphus antiquus (Gmelin)
Resident

*203. Japanese Murrelet
  Synthliboramphus wumizusume (Temminck)
  Resident
*204. Rhinoceros Auklet
  Cerorhinca monocerata (Pallas)
  Winter visitor

ORDER COLUMBIFORMES

Family Pteroclididae

*205. Pallas' Sandgrouse
  Syrrhaptes paradoxus (Pallas)
  Accidentals and strays

Family Columbidae

206. Rock Dove
  Columba rupestris rupestris (Pallas)
  Resident
207. Japanese Wood Pigeon
  Columba janthina janthina (Temminck)
  Resident
*208. Collared Turtle Dove
  Streptopelia decaocto decaocto (Freivaldszky)
  Resident
209. Rufous Turtle Dove
  Streptopelia orientalis orientalis (Latham)
  Resident
*210. Japanese Green Pigeon
  Sphenurus siboldii siboldii (Temminck)
  Accidentals and strays

ORDER CUCULIFORMES

Family Cuculidae

*211. Horsfieldis Hawk-Cuckoo
 Cuculus fugax hyperythrus (Gould)
 Summer visitor
*212. Indian Cuckoo
 Cuculus micropterus micropterus (Gould)
 Summer visitor
 213. Common Cuckoo
 Cuculus canorus telephonus (Heine)
 Summer visitor
*214. Oriental Cuckoo
 Cuculus saturatus horsfieldi (Moore)
 Summer visitor
 215. Little Cuckoo
 Cuculus poliocephalus poliocephalus (Latham)
 Summer visitor

ORDER STRIGIFORMES

Family Strigidae

*216. Snowy Owl
 Nyctea scandiaca (Linné)
 Accidentals and strays
 217. Eagle Owl
 Bubo bubo kiautschensis (Reichenow)
 Resident
 218. Long-eared Owl
 Asio otus otus (Linné)
 Resident
 219. Short-eared Owl
 Asio flammeus flammeus (Pontoppidan)
 Winter visitor
 220. Scops Owl
 Otus scops stictonotus (Sharpe)

Summer visitor
221. Collared Scops Owl
Otus bakkamoena ussuriensis (Buturlin)
Winter visitor
222. Brown Hawk Owl
Ninox scutulata (Raffles)
Summer visitor
*223. Ural Owl
Strix uralensis nikolskii (Buturlin)
Accidentals and strays
224. Korean Wood Owl
Strix aluco ma (Clark)
Resident
*225. Little Owl
Athene noctua plumipes (Swinhoe)
Summer visitor

ORDER CAPRIMULGIFORMES

Family Caprimulgidae

*226. Jungle Nightjar
Caprimulgus indicus jodaka (Temminck & Schlegel)
Summer visitor

ORDER APODIFORMES

Family Apodidae

*227. White-throated Needle-tailed Swift
Chaetura caudacuta caudacuta (Latham)
Transient
228. White-rumped Swift
Apus pacificus pacificus (Latham)
Summer visitor

ORDER CORACIIFORMES

Family Alcedinidae

*229. Greater Pied Kingfisher
  Ceryle lugubris lugubris (Temminck)
  Winter visitor
230. Black-capped Kingfisher
  Halcyon pileata (Boddaert)
  Summer visitor
231. Ruddy Kingfisher
  Halcyon coromanda major (Temminck & Schlegel)
  Summer visitor
232. Common Kingfisher
  Alcedo atthis bengalensis (Gmelin)
  Summer visitor

Family Coraciidae

233. Broad-billed Roller
  Eurystomus orientalis calonyx (Sharpe)
  Summer visitor

Family Upupidae

234. Hoopoe
  Upupa epops saturata (Lönnberg)
  Summer visitor

ORDER PICIFORMES

Family picidae

*235. Wryneck
  Jynx torquilla chinensis (Hesse)

Winter visitor
236. Gray-headed Woodpecker
 Picus canus griseoviridis (Clark)
 Resident
237. Black Woodpecker
 Dryocopus martius (Linné)
 Resident
238. White-bellied Black Woodpecker
 Dryocopus javensis richardsi (Tristram)
 Resident
239. Great Spotted Woodpecker
 Dendrocopos major hondoensis (Kuroda)
 Resident
240. White-backed Woodpecker
 Dendrocopos leucotos leucotos (Bechstein)
 Resident
*241. Rufous-bellied Pied Woodpecker
 Dendrocopos hyperythrus subrufinus (Cabanis & Heine)
 Accidentals and strays
242. Dagelet White-backed Woodpecker
 Dendrocopos leucotos takahashii (Kuroda & Mori)
 Resident
243. Gray-headed Pygmy Woodpecker
 Dendrocopos canicapillus doerriesi (Hargitt)
 Resident
*244. Japanese Pygmy Woodpecker
 Dendrocopos kizuki ijimae (Taka-tsukasa)
 Resident

ORDER PASSERIFORMES

Family Pittidae

245. Fairy Pitta
 Pitta brachyuro nympha (Temminck & Schlegel)
 Summer visitor

Family Alaudidae

*246. Crested Lark
   Galerida cristata coreensis (Taczanowski)
   Resident
*247. Short-toed Lark
   Calandrella rufescens cheleensis (Swinhoe)
   Transient
 248. Skylark
   Alauda arvensis (Linné)
   Resident

Family Hirundinidae

 249. Bank Swallow
   Riparia riparia ijimae (Lönnberg)
   Transient
 250. House Swallow
   Hirundo rustica gutturalis (Scopoli)
   Summer visitor
 251. Red-rumped Swallow
   Hirundo daurica japonica (Temminck & Schlegel)
   Summer visitor
*252. House Martin
   Delichon urbica dasypus (Bonaparte)
   Transient

Family Motacillidae

 253. Forest Wagtail
   Dendronanthus indicus (Gmelin)
   Summer visitor
 254. Yellow Wagtail
   Motacilla flava taivana (Swinnhoe)
   Transient
*255. Siberia Yellow Wagtail
   Motacilla flava simillima (Hartert)

Transient
256. Gray Wagtail
    Motacilla cinerea robusta (Brehm)
    Summer visitor
257. White-faced Wagtail
    Motacilla alba leucopsis (Gould)
    Summer visitor
258. White Wagtail
    Motacilla alba lugens (Gloger)
    Winter visitor
259. Pied Wagtail
    Motacilla alba ocularis (Swinhoe)
    Transient
260. Japanese Wagtail
    Motacilla grandis (Sharpe)
    Summer visitor
*261. Richard's Pipit
    Anthus novaeseelandiae sinensis (Bonaparte)
    Transient
*262. Godlewski's Pipit
    Anthus godlewskii (Taczanowski)
    Transient
263. Indian Tree Pipit
    Anthus hodgsoni hodgsoni (Richmond)
    Transient
*264. Pechora Pipit
    Anthus gustavi gustavi (Swinhoe)
    Transient
*265. Red-throated Pipit
    Anthus cervinus (Pallas)
    Transient
*266. Hodgson's Pipit
    Anthus roseatus (Blyth)
    Transient
267. Water Pipit
    Anthus spinoletta japonicus (Temminck & Schlegel)
    Winter visitor

Family Campephagidae

*268. Ashy Minivet
Pericrocotus divaricatus divaricatus (Raffles)
Summer visitor

Family Pycnonotidae

269. Brown-eared Bulbul
Hypsipetes amaurotis hensoni (Stejneger)
Resident

Family Laniidae

270. Thick-billed Shrike
Lanius tigrinus (Drapiez)
Summer visitor
271. Bull-headed Shrike
Lanius bucephalus bucephalus (Temminck & Schlegel)
Resident
272. Brown Shrike
Lanius cristatus lucionensis (Linné)
Summer visitor
273. Northern Shrike
Lanius excubitor bianchii (Hartert)
Winter visitor
*274. Chinese Great Gray Shrike
Lanius sphenocercus sphenocercus (Cabanis)
Winter visitor

Family Bombycillidae

275. Bohemian Waxwing
Bombycilla garrulus centralasiae (Poliakov)
Winter visitor
276. Japanese Waxwing
Bombycilla japonica (Siebold)

Winter visitor

Family Cinclidae

*277. Brown Dipper
 Cinclus pallasii pallasii (Temminck)
 Resident

Family Troglodytidae

278. Winter Wren
 Troglodytes troglodytes dauricus (Dybowski & Taczanowski)
 Resident

Family Prunellidae

*279. Alpine Accentor
 Prunella collaris erythropygia (Swinhoe)
 Resident
*280. Siberian Accentor
 Prunella montanella badia (Portenko)
 Winter visitor

Family Muscicapidae

Subfamily Turdinae

*281. Japanese Robin
 Erithacus akahige akahige (Temminck)
 Accidentals and strays
*282. Swinhoe's Red-tailed Robin
 Erithacus sibilans (Swinhoe)
 Transient
*283. Siberian Rubythroat
 Erithacus calliope (Pallas)
 Transient

*284. Bluethroat
   Erithacus svecicus svecicus (Linné)
   Winter visitor
*285. Siberian Blue Robin
   Erithacus cyane (Pallas)
   Transient
 286. Siberian Bluechat
   Tarsiger cyanurus cyanurus (Pallas)
   Transient
 287. Pied Wheatear
   Oenanthe pleschanka
   Accidentals and strays
 288. Daurian Redstart
   Phoenicurus auroreus auroreus (Pallas)
   Resident
 289. Stonechat
   Saxicola torquata stejnegeri (Parrot)
   Summer visitor
 290. Bule Rockthrush
   Monticola solitarius philippensis (Müller)
   Resident
*291. White-breasted Rockthrush
   Monticola gularis (Swinhoe)
   Transient
*292. Siberian Thrush
   Turdus sibiricus davisoni (Hume)
   Transient
 293. White's Ground Thrush
   Turdus dauma aureus (Holandre)
   Summer visitor
 294. Gray-backed Thrush
   Turdus hortulorum (Sclater)
   Summer visitor
*295. Gray Thrush
   Turdus cardis (Temminck)
   Accidentals and stranger
*296. Brown Thrush

Turdus chrysolaus (Temminck)
Transient
297. Pale Thrush
   Turdus pallidus (Gmelin)
   Summer visitor
*298. Gray-headed Thrush
   Turdus obscurus (Gmelin)
   Transient
299. Dusky Thrush
   Turdus naumanni eunomus (Temminck)
   Winter visitor
300. Naumann's Thrush
   Turdus naumanni naumanni (Temminck)
   Winter visitor

Subfamily Paradoxornithnae

301. Vinous-throated Parrotbill
   Paradoxornis webbiana fulvicauda (Campbell)
   Resident

Subfamily Timaliinae

*302. White-browed Chinese Babbler
   Rhopophilus pekinensis pekinensis (Swinhoe)
   Winter visitor

Subfamily Sylviinae

*303. Short-tailed Bush Warbler
   Cettia Squameiceps (Swinhoe)
   Summer visitor
304. Bush Warbler
   Cettia diphone borealis (Campbell)
   Summer visitor
*305. Quelpart Bush Warbler
   Cettia diphone cantans (Temminck & Schlegel)

Summer visitor
- *306. Japanese Marsh Warbler
  Megalurus pryeri pryeri (Seebohm)
  Accidentals and strays
- *307. Gray's Grasshopper Warbler
  Locustella fasciolata (Gray)
  Transient
- *308. Middendorff's Grasshopper Warbler
  Locustella ochotensis ochotensis (Middendorff)
  Transient
- 309. Island Grasshopper Warbler
  Locustella ochotensis pleski (Taczanowski)
  Summer visitor
- *310. Pallas' Grasshopper Warbler
  Locustella certhiola certhiola (Pallas)
  Transient
- *311. Lanceolated Grasshopper Warbler
  Locustella lanceolata (Temminck)
  Summer visitor
- *312. Lesser Whitethroat
  Sylvia curruca (Linné)
  Accidentals and strays
- *313. Black-browed Reed Warbler
  Acrocephalus bistrigiceps (Swinhoe)
  Transient
- *314. Thick-billed Reed Warbler
  Acrocephalus aedon (Pallas)
  Transient
- 315. Great Reed Warbler
  Acrocephalus arundinaceus orientalis (Temminck & Schlegel)
  Summer visitor
- *316. Radde's Willow Warbler
  Phylloscopus schwarzi (Radde)
  Transient
- *317. Yellow-browed Warbler
  Phylloscopus inornatus inornatus (Blyth)

Transient
*318. Pallas Willow Warbler
Phylloscopus proregulus proregulus (Pallas)
Transient
319. Arctic Warbler
Phylloscopus borealis xanthodryas (Swinhoe)
Transient
*320. Greenish Warbler
Phylloscopus trochiloides plumbeitarsus (Swinhoe)
Transient
321. Pale-legged Willow Warbler
Phylloscopus tenellipes (Swinhoe)
Transient
*322. Crowned Willow Warbler
Phylloscopus occipitalis coronatus (Temminck & Schlegel)
Summer visitor
*323. Goldcrest
Regulus regulus japonensis (Blakistion)
Winter visitor
*324. Fan-tailed Warbler
Cisticola juncidis brunniceps (Temminck & Schlegel)
Summer visitor

Subfamily Muscicapinae

325. Tricolor Flycatcher
Ficedula zanthopygia (Hay)
Summer visitor
*326. Narcissus Flycatcher
Ficedula narcissina narcissina (Temminck)
Transient
*327. Mugimaki Flycatcher
Ficedula mugimaki (Temminck)
Transient
*328. Red-breasted Flycatcher
Ficedula parva albicilla (Pallas)

Transient
329. Blue and White Flycatcher
    Cyanoptila cyanomelana cyanomelana (Temminck)
    Summer visitor
*330. Sooty Flycatcher
    Muscicapa sibirica sibirica (Gmelin)
    Transient
*331. Gray-spotted Flycatcher
    Muscicapa griseisticta (Swinhoe)
    Transient
*332. Brown Flycatcher
    Muscicapa latirostris (Raffles)
    Transient

Subfamily Monarchinae

*333. Black Paradise Flycatcher
    Terpsiphone atrocaudata atrocaudata (Eyton)
    Summer visitor

Family Aegithalidae

334. Long-tailed Tit
    Aegithalos caudatus magnus (Clark)
    Resident

Family Remizidae

*335. Penduline Tit
    Remiz pendulinus consobrinus (Swinhoe)
    Winter visitor

Family Paridae

336. Marsh Tit
    Parus palustris hellmayri (Bianchi)
    Resident

337. Coal Tit
    Parus ater amurensis (Buturlin)
    Resident
338. Varied Tit
    Parus varius varius (Temminck & Schlegel)
    Resident
339. Great Tit
    Parus major minor (Temminck & Schlegel)
    Resident

Family Sittidae

340. Nuthatch
    Sitta europaea amurensis (Swinhoe)
    Resident
*341. Chinese Nuthatch
    Sitta villosa villosa (Verreaux)
    Accidentals and stranger

Family Certhiidae

*342. Tree Creeper
    Certhia familliaris orientalis (Demaniewski)
    Winter visitor

Family Zosteropidae

343. Japanese White-eye
    Zosterops japonica japonica (Temminck & Schlegel)
    Resident
*344. Chestnut-flanked White-eye
    Zosterops erythropleura (Swinhoe)
    Accidentals and stranger

Family Emberizidae

*345. Pine Bunting

Emberiza Leucocephala leucocephala (Gmelin)
Winter visitor

346. Siberian Meadow Bunting
Emberiza cioides castaneiceps (Moore)
Resident

347. Japanese Reed Bunting
Emberiza yessoensis continentalis (Witherby)
Winter visitor

348. Tristram's Bunting
Emberiza tristrami (Swinhoe)
Transient

349. Gray-headed Bunting
Emberiza fucata fucata (Pallas)
Summer visitor

350. Little Bunting
Emberiza pusilla (Pallas)
Transient

*351. Yellow-browed Bunting
Emberiza chrysophrys (Pallas)
Transient

352. Rustic Bunting
Emberiza rustica latifascia (Portenko)
Winter visitor

353. Yellow-throated Bunting
Emberiza elegans elegans (Temminck)
Resident

*354. Yellow-breasted Bunting
Emberiza aureola ornata (Shulpin)
Transient

355. Chestnut Bunting
Emberiza rutila (Pallas)
Transient

*356. Japanese Yellow Bunting
Emberiza sulphurata (Temminck & Schlegel)
Transient

357. Siberia Black-faced Bunting
Emberiza spodocephala spodocephala (Pallas)

Transient
* 358. Black-faced Bunting
    Emberiza spodocephala personata (Temminck)
    Transient
* 359. Gray Bunting
    Emberiza variabilis (Temminck)
    Accidentals and strays
* 360. Pallas Reed Bunting
    Emberiza pallasi polaris (Middendorff)
    Winter visitor
  361. Reed Bunting
    Emberiza schoeniclus pyrrhulina (Swinhoe)
    Winter visitor
* 362. Lapland Longspur
    Calcarius lapponicus coloratus (Ridgway)
    Transient
* 363. Snow Bunting
    Plectrophenax nivalis vlasowae (Portenko)
    Accidentals and stranger

Family Fringillidae

  364. Brambling
    Fringilla montifringilla (Linné)
    Winter visitor
  365. Oriental Greenfinch
    Carduelis sinica ussuriensis (Hartert)
    Resident
* 366. Japanese Greenfinch
    Carduelis sinica minor (Temminck & Schlegel)
    Resident
  367. Siskin
    Carduelis spinus (Linné)
    Winter visitor
* 368. Common Redpoll
    Acanthis flammea flammea (Linné)
    Winter visitor

*369. Rosy Finch
   Leucosticte arctoa brunneonucha (Brandt)
   Winter visitor
370. Scarlet Finch
   Carpodacus erythrinus grebnitskii (Stejneger)
   Accidentals and strays
371. Pallas' Rosy Finch
   Carpodacus roseus (Pallas)
   Winter visitor
*372. Red Crossbill
   Loxia curvirostra japonica (Ridgway)
   Winter visitor
*373. White-winged Grossbill
   Loxia leucoptera bifasciata (Brehm)
   Accidentals and strays
374. Long-tailed Rose Finch
   Uragus sibiricus ussurensis (Buturlin)
   Winter visitor
375. Bullfinch
   Pyrrhula pyrrhula rosacea (Seebohm)
   Winter visitor
*376. *Pyrrhula pyrrhula cassinii* (Baird)
   Winter visitor
377. Chinese Grosbeak
   Eophona migratoria migratoria (Hartert)
   Summer visitor
*378. Japanese Grosbeak
   Eophona personata magnirostris (Hartert)
   Winter visitor
379. Hawfinch
   Coccothraustes coccothraustes coccothraustes (Linné)
   Winter visitor

Family Ploceidae

380. Russet Sparrow
   Passer rutilans rutilans (Temminck)

Resident
381. Tree Sparrow
Passer montanus dybowskii (Domaniewski)
Resident

Family Sturnidae

382. Daurian Myna
Sturnus sturninus (Pallas)
Summer visitor
*383. Red-cheeked Myna
Sturnus philippensis (Forster)
Summer visitor
*384. Gray-backed Myna
Sturnus sinensis (Gmelin)
Accidentals and strays
385. Gray Starling
Sturnus cineraceus (Temminck)
Summer visitor

Family Oriolidae

386. Black-naped Oriole
Oriolus chinensis diffusus (Sharpe)
Summer visitor

Family Dicruridae

*387. Black Drongo
Dicrurus macrocercus harterti (Stuary Baker)
Accidentals and stranger
*388. Spangled Drongo
Dicrurus hottentottus brevirostris (Cabanis)
accidentals and strays

Family Corvidae

389. Jay
    Garrulus glandarius brandtii (Eversmann)
    Resident
390. Azure-winged Magpie
    Cyanopica cyanus koreensis (Pallas)
    Resident
391. Black-billed Magpie
    Pica pica sericea (Gould)
    Resident
*392. Nutcracker
    Nucifraga caryocatactes macrorhynchos (Brehm)
    Resident
*393. Jackdaw
    Corvus monedula dauricus (Pallas)
    Winter visitor
*394. Rook
    Corvus frugilegus pastinator (Gould)
    Winter visitor
395. Carrion Crow
    Corvus corone orientalis (Eversmann)
    Resident
*396. Jungle Crow
    Corvus macrorhynchos mandshuricus (Buturlin)
    Resident

Scientific Names

Accipiter soloensis 145
Acrocephalus arundinaceus 378
Aegithalos caudatus 385
Aegypius monachus 151
Aguila chrysaetos 150
Aix galericulata 108
Alauda arvensis 317
Alcedo atthis 292
Amaurornis phoenicurus 175
Anas acuta 115
Anas americana 119
Anas clypeata 100
Anas crecca 102
Anas falcata 112
Anas formosa 105
Anas penelope 117
Anas platyrhynchos 92
Anas poecilorhyncha 96
Anas querquedula 104
Anas strepera 114
Anser albifrons 74
Anser cygnoides 76
Anser fabalis 77
Anthus hodgsoni 337
Anthus spinoletta 338
Apus pacificus 288
Aquila heliaca 149
Ardea cinerea 59
Arenaria interpres 198
Asio flammeus 283
Asio otus 282
Aythya ferina 120

Aythya fuligula 122
Aythya marila 125
Bombycilla garrulus 350
Bombycilla japonica 352
Botaurus stellaris 31
Branta bernicla 71
Bubo bubo 278
Bubulcus ibis 40
Bucephala clangula 134
Butastur indicus 148
Buteo buteo 146
Butorides striatus 38
Calidris acuminata 203
Calidris alpina 204
Calidris ferruginea 206
Calidris minutilla 202
Calidris ruficollis 200
Calidris tenuirostris 207
Calonectris leucomelas 23
Carduelis sinica 416
Carduelis spinus 419
Carpodacus erythrinus 420
Carpodacus roseus 421
Cettia diphone 375
Charadrius alexandrinus 190
Charadrius dubius 186
Charadrius mongolus 192
Charadrius placidus 189
Ciconia ciconia 64
Circus aeruginosus 155
Circus cyaneus 153
Circus melanoleucos 154

Coccothraustes coccothraustes 428
Columba janthina 269
Columba rupestris 267
Corvus corone 451
Corvus frugilegus 450
Crocethia alba 209
Cuculus canorus 274
Cuculus poliocephalus 276
Cyanopica cyana 443
Cyanoptila cyanomelana ... 384
Cygnus columbianus 87
Cygnus cygnus 82
Cygnus olor 79
Dendrocopos canicapillus ... 312
Dendrocopos kizuki 314
Dendrocopos leucotos 308
Dendrocopos leucotos takahashii 310
Dendrocopos major 307
Dendronanthus indicus ... 325
Dryocopus javensis 304
Dryocopus martius 301
Egretta alba 52
Egretta eulophotes 42
Egretta garzetta 45
Egretta intermedia 48
Egretta sacra 56
Emberiza cioides 398
Emberiza elegans 408
Emberiza fucata 403
Emberiza pusilla 405
Emberiza rustica 406
Emberiza rutila 410
Emberiza schoeniclus 413
Emberiza spodocephala 412

Emberiza tristrami 401
Emberiza yessoensis 400
Eophona migratoria 425
Eurystomus orientalis calonyx 295
Falco peregrinus 156
Falco tinnunculus 157
Ficedula zanthopygia 382
Fringilla montifringilla ... 414
Fulica atra 181
Gallicrex cinerea 179
Gallinago gallinago 238
Gallinula chloropus 176
Garrulus glandarius 441
Gavia pacifica 13
Gavia stellata 12
Glareola maldivarum 243
Grus japonensis 163
Grus monacha 170
Grus vipio 166
Haematopus ostralegus 183
Halcyon coromanda 290
Halcyon pileata 289
Haliaeetus albicilla 142
Haliaeetus pelagicus 143
Himantopus himantopus ... 240
Hirundo daurica 323
Hirundo rustica 319
Histrionicus histrionicus ... 132
Hypsipetes amaurotis 340
Ixobrychus sinensis 33
Lanius bucephalus 345
Lanius cristatus 347
Lanius excubitor 348
Lanius tigrinus 343
Larus argentatus 248

Larus crassirostris 252	*Passer rutilans* 429
Larus ridibundus 245	*Phalacrocorax filamentosus* 28
Larus schistisagus 250	*Phalacrocorax pelagicus* 30
Larus tridactylus 257	*Phalaropus lobatus* 242
Limicola falcinellus 212	*Phasianus colchicus* 160
Limosa lapponica 230	*Phoenicurus auroreus* 359
Limosa limosa 228	*Phylloscopus borealis* 380
Locustella ochotensis pleski 377	*Phylloscopus occipitalis* 381
Melanitta fusca 130	*Pica pica* 415
Melanitta nigra 129	*Picus canus* 300
Mergus albellus 135	*Pitta brachyura* 316
Mergus merganser 139	*Platalea leucorodia* 68
Mergus serrator 137	*Platalea minor* 70
Monticola solitarius 364	*Pluvialis dominica* 194
Motacilla alba leucopsis ... 330	*Pluvialis squatarola* 195
Motacilla alba lugens 333	*Podiceps cristatus* 20
Motacilla alba ocularis 334	*Podiceps grisegena* 22
Motacilla cinerea 328	*Podiceps nigricollis* 18
Motacilla flava taivana 326	*Podiceps ruficollis* 16
Motacilla grandis 335	*Porzana fusca* 174
Ninox scutulata 286	*Pyrrhula pyrrhula* 424
Numenius madagascariensis 232	*Riparia riparia* 318
	Saxicola ferrea 358
Numenius phaeopus 234	*Saxicola torquata* 362
Nycticorax nycticorax 35	*Sitta europaea* 392
Oceanodroma monorhis 26	*Sterna albifrons* 262
Oriolus chinensis 438	*Sterna hirundo* 260
Otus bakkamoena 285	*Streptopelia orientalis* 271
Otus scops 284	*Strix aluco* 287
Pandion haliaetus 141	*Sturnus cineraceus* 435
Paradoxornis webbiana 372	*Sturnus sturninus* 433
Parus ater 387	*Synthliboramphus antiquus* 265
Parus major 390	*Tadorna ferruginea* 88
Parus palustris 386	*Tadorna tadorna* 89
Parus varius 388	*Tarsiger cyanurus* 356
Passer montanus 431	*Tetrastes bonasia* 158

Tringa brevipes 221
Tringa erythropus 213
Tringa glareola 220
Tringa hypoleucos 223
Tringa nebularia 218
Tringa stagnatilis 217
Tringa totanus 216
Troglodytes troglodytes 354
Turdus dauma 365
Turdus hortulorum 366
Turdus naumanni eunomus 368
Turdus naumanni naumanni 370
Turdus pallidus 367
Upupa epops 297
Uragus sibiricus 423
Vanellus vanellus 196
Xenus cinereus 225
Zosterops japonica 394

English Names

American Wigeon	119
Ancient Murrelet	265
Arctic Warbler	380
Australian Curlew	232
Azure-winged Magpie	443
Baikal Teal	105
Bank Swallow	318
Bar-tailed Godwit	230
Bean Goose	77
Bittern	31
Black-bellied Plover	195
Black-billed Magpie	445
Black-capped Kingfisher	289
Black-crowned Night Heron	35
Black-faced Spoonbill	70
Black-headed Gull	245
Black-legged Kittiwake	257
Black-naped Oriole	438
Black Scoter	129
Black-tailed Godwit	228
Black-tailed Gull	252
Black Vulture	151
Black-winged Stilt	240
Black Woodpecker	301
Blue and White Flycatcher	384
Blue Rockthrush	364
Bohemian Waxwing	350
Brambling	414
Brant	71
Broad-billed Roller	295
Broad-billed Sandpiper	212
Brown-eared Bulbul	340
Brown Hawk Owl	286
Brown Shrike	347
Bullfinch	424
Bull-headed Shrike	345
Bush Warbler	375
Carrion Crow	451
Cattle Egret	40
Chestnut Bunting	410
Chinese Egret	42
Chinese Grosbeak	425
Chinese Little Bittern	33
Chinese Sparrow Hawk	145
Coal Tit	387
Collared Scops Owl	285
Common Buzzard	146
Common Cuckoo	274
Common Gallinule	176
Common Goldeneye	134
Common Kingfisher	292
Common Merganser	139
Common Sandpiper	223
Common Shelduck	89
Common Snipe	238
Common Tern	260
Coot	181
Crowned Willow Warbler	381
Curlew Sandpiper	206
Dagelet White-backed Woodpecker	310
Daurian Myna	433
Daurian Redstart	359
Dunlin	204
Dusky Thrush	368
Eagle Owl	278
Eared Grebe	18
Eastern Reef Heron	56

Fairy Pitta	316	Indian Pratincole	243
Falcated Teal	112	Indian Tree Pipit	337
Forest Wagtail	325	Intermediate Egret	48
Gadwall	114	Island Grasshopper Warbler	377
Garganey	104	Japanese Pygmy Woodpecker	314
Golden Eagel	150	Japanese Reed Bunting	400
Gray-backed Thrush	366	Japanese Wagtail	335
Gray Bushchat	358	Japanese Waxwing	352
Gray-faced Buzzard-Eagle	148	Japanese White-eye	394
Gray-headed Bunting	403	Japanese Wood Pigeon	269
Gray-headed Pygmy Woodpecker	312	Jay	441
Gray-headed Woodpecker	300	Kentish Plover	190
Gray Heron	59	Kestrel	157
Gray Starling	435	Korean Wood Owl	287
Gray-tailed Tattler	221	Lapwing	196
Gray Wagtail	328	Lesser Golden Plover	194
Great Crested Grebe	20	Little Bunting	405
Great Egret	52	Little Cuckoo	276
Greater Scaup	125	Little Egret	45
Great Knot	207	Little Grebe	16
Great Reed Warbler	378	Little Ringed Plover	186
Great Spotted Woodpecker	307	Little Tern	262
Great Tit	390	Long-billed Ringed Plover	189
Green-backed Heron	38	Long-eared Owl	282
Greenshank	218	Long-tailed Rose Finch	423
Harlequin Duck	132	Long-tailed Tit	385
Hawfinch	428	Long-toed Stint	202
Hazel Grouse	158	Mallard	92
Herring Gull	248	Manchurian Crane	163
Hooded Crane	170	Mandarin Duck	108
Hoopoe	297	Marsh Harrier	155
House Swallow	319	Marsh Sandpiper	217
Imperial Eagle	149	Marsh Tit	386
		Mongolian Plover	192

Mute Swan	79	Rustic Bunting	406
Naumann's Thrush	370	Sanderling	209
Northern Harrier	153	Scarlet Finch	420
Northern Phalarope	242	Scops Owl	284
Northern Shrike	348	Sharp-tailed Sandpiper	203
Nuthatch	392	Short-eared Owl	283
Oriental Greenfinch	416	Shoveller	100
Osprey	141	Siberian Black-faced Bunting	412
Oystercatcher	183	Siberian Bluechat	356
Pacific Diver	13	Siberian Meadow Bunting	398
Pale Thrush	367	Siskin	419
Pallas' Rosy Finch	421	Skylark	317
Pelagic Cormorant	30	Slaty-backed Gull	250
Peregrine Falcon	156	Smew	135
Pied Harrier	154	Spoonbill	68
Pied Wagtail	334	Spot-billed Duck	96
Pintail	115	Spotted Redshank	213
Pochard	120	Steller's Sea-Eagle	143
Red-breasted Merganser	137	Stonechat	362
Red-necked Grebe	22	Streaked Shearwater	23
Red-rumped Swallow	323	Swan Goose	76
Redshank	216	Swinhoe's Storm Petrel	26
Red-throated Diver	12	Teal	102
Reed Bunting	413	Temminck's Cormorant	28
Ring-necked Pheasant	160	Terex Sandpiper	225
Rock Dove	267	Thick-billed Shrike	343
Rook	450	Tree Sparrow	431
Ruddy Crake	174	Tricolor Flycatcher	382
Ruddy Kingfisher	290	Tristram's Bunting	401
Ruddy Shelduck	88	Tufted Duck	122
Ruddy Turnstone	198	Varied Tit	388
Rufous-necked Stint	200	Vinous-throated Parrotbill	372
Rufous Turtle Dove	271	Watercock	179
Russet Sparrow	429	Water Pipit	338

Whimbrel ················· 234	White-tailed Eagle ········ 142
Whistling Swan ············ 87	White Wagtail ············· 333
White-backed Woodpecker ··· 308	White-winged Scoter ······· 130
White-bellied Black Woodpecker ················· 304	White's Ground Thrush ····· 365
White-breasted Waterhen ···· 175	Whooper Swan ············· 82
White-faced Wagtail ········ 330	Wigeon ··················· 117
White-fronted Goose ········ 74	Winter Wren ·············· 354
White-naped Crane ········· 166	Wood Sandpiper ··········· 220
White-rumped Swift ········ 288	Yellow-throated Bunting ···· 408
White Stork ··············· 64	Yellow Wagtail ············ 326

References

- Long, A.J. et al. *A Survey of Coastal Wetlands and Shorebirds in South Korea, Spring 1988*. AWB Pub., Kuala Lumpur, Malaysia, 1988.
- Parish, D. *Conservation of Wader Habitats in East Aisa.* Wader Study Group Bull, No. 49, Suppl, IWRB Spec Pub., No. 7, 1987.
- Recher, H.F. *Some Aspects of Ecology of Migrant Shorebirds.* Ecology 47, 1966.
- Swennen, C. et al. *Study of Intertidal Benthos in South Korea 1989.* AWB Pub., Kuala Lumpur, Malaysia, 1990.
- Pyong-oh, Won. *The Birds of Korea.* Kyo-hak Publishing Co., 1993.
- Moo-Boo, Yoon. *Reports on the Survey of the Natural Environment in Korea.* Vol. 2, Seoul : The Preservation of Nature Association, 1982.
- Moo-Boo, Yoon. *Reports on the Survey of the Natural Environment in Korea.* Vol. 3, Seoul : The Preservation of Nature Association, 1983.
- Moo-Boo, Yoon. Hyeok-Doo, Kwon *Reports on the Survey of the Natural Environment in Korea,* Vol. 6, Seoul : The Preservation of Nature Association, 1987.
- Moo-Boo, Yoon. *A New Checklist of Korean Birds.* Academy Publishing Co., 1988.
- Moo-Boo, Yoon. Hyeok-Doo, Kwon. *Reports on the Survey of the Natural Environment in Korea.* Vol. 7, Seoul : The Preservation of Nature Association, 1987.
- Moo-Boo, Yoon. *Birds of Korea,* Seoul : Academy Publishing Co., 1988.
- Moo-Boo, Yoon. *Birds of Kangwon Province.* Kangwon Province : Kangwon Provincial Education Committee, 1988.
- Moo-Boo, Yoon. *Korean Resident Birds.* Seoul : Dae Won Sa, 1990.
- Moo-Boo, Yoon. *Korean Migratory Birds.* Seoul : Dae Won Sa, 1990.

Moo-Boo Yoon

Prof. Yoon was born on Kŏje Island in Kyŏngsangnam Province in 1941. He received his B.S. in biology from Kyŏnghee University in 1963 and his masters from the same university in 1967. He is now on the Advisory Committee on Animal Life to the Seoul City Government Concerning his specialty, birds, to the Ministry of Culture and Information on cultural properties, and to the Ministry of Construction on of Han River wildlife protection. Prof. Yoon is now a Professor in the Department of Biology of his alma mater.

He has published many books and articles including: *Korean Bird Songs, Ecology and Pictures of Korean Birds, The Natural History of Kangwon Province, The Latest Checklist of Korean Birds, Resident Korean Birds, Migratory Korean Birds.*

Wild Birds of Korea
by Moo-Boo Yoon
Published by Kyo-Hak Publishing Co.
105-65 Kongdŭk-dong, Map'o-gu, Seoul, Korea.
Tel. 312-6685, 718-8882
Printed in Korea.
First Edition in English 1995.

·$40
ISBN 89-09-01669-8 96490